POCKET

SAN FRANCISCO

TOP EXPERIENCES · LOCAL LIFE

ASHLEY HARRELL
ALISON BING

Contents

Van Ness Avenue and Market Street cable car
MATTEO COLOMBO / GETTY IMAGES ©

Special Features

COVID-19

We have re-checked every business in this book before publication to ensure that it is still open after the COVID-19 outbreak. However, the economic and social impacts of COVID-19 will continue to be felt long after the outbreak has been contained, and many businesses, services and events referenced in this guide may experience ongoing restrictions. Some businesses may be temporarily closed, have changed their opening hours and services, or require bookings; some unfortunately could have closed permanently. We suggest you check with venues before visiting for the latest information.

San Francisco's Top Experiences

Marvel at the Golden Gate Bridge
San Francisco's art-deco icon. **p34**

RICOWDE / GETTY IMAGES ©

FLIPHOTO / SHUTTERSTOCK ©

Escape to Alcatraz

San Francisco's most famous sight. **p32**

RAFAEL RAMIREZ LEE / SHUTTERSTOCK ©

Meander Through Golden Gate Park

SF's mile-wide, 3-mile-long wild streak. **p164**

WENDY CONNETT / ALAMY STOCK PHOTO ©

Check Out the Thought-Provoking Mission Murals

Pride and protest mark Mission streets. **p112**

Discover Local History at the Cable Car Museum
Steampunk peak technology in action. **p94**

SUTTER ST.
POLK & **54** LARKIN
OAKLAND FERRIES.

WONDERLUSTPICSTRAVEL / SHUTTERSTOCK ©

MICHAEL WARWICK / SHUTTERSTOCK ©

Trawl the Market Stalls at the Ferry Building

Skip the ferry and dine here. **p54**

Survey the City from Coit Tower

SF's scandalous art-deco landmark. **p74**

JEFFREY B BANKE / SHUTTERSTOCK © ARCHITECT ARTHUR BROWN JR

Take in the Sea Air at Fisherman's Wharf

San Francisco's epicenter of tourism. **p46**

Explore the San Francisco Museum of Modern Art

Expanding artistic horizons since 1935. **p56**

BENNY MARTY / SHUTTERSTOCK ©

GADO IMAGES / GETTY IMAGES ©

Revisit the '60s on Haight Street

Feel the Flower Power. **p148**

Dining Out

Other US cities boast bigger monuments, but San Francisco packs more flavor. Chef Alice Waters set the Bay Area standard for organic, sustainable, seasonal food back in 1971 at Chez Panisse, and today you'll find California's pasture-raised meats and organic produce featured on the Bay Area's trendsetting, cross-cultural menus.

Farmers Markets

NorCal idealists who headed back to the land in the 1970s started the nation's organic-farming movement. Today the local bounty can be sampled across San Francisco, the US city with the most farmers markets per capita.

Fine Dining

Reservations are a must at popular San Francisco restaurants. Most take online reservations through their websites or OpenTable (www.opentable.com), but if the system shows no availability, call the restaurant directly – some seats may be held for phone reservations and early-evening walk-ins, and there may be last-minute cancellations or room at the bar. Small, celebrated SF bistros like Benu (p64), Rich Table (p155), State Bird Provisions (p104) and Frances (p141) offer limited seating, so call a month ahead and take what's available.

Food Trucks & Carts

SF's largest gathering of gourmet trucks is Off the Grid (p42), which hosts several events weekly. Sunday brings OTG picnics to the Presidio and Friday sees 30-plus food trucks circle their wagons in Fort Mason. You can track food trucks at Roaming Hunger (www.roaminghunger.com/sf/vendors).

ANDREW MONTGOMERY / LONELY PLANET ©

Best NorCal Cuisine

Rich Table Tasty, inventive California fare with French fine-dining finesse makes you feel clever by association. (p155)

Al's Place California dreams are shared here, with imaginative plates of pristine seafood and seasonal specialties. (p122)

Mister Jiu's Bringing honest ingredients and wild creativity to the table inside a historic Chinatown banquet hall. (p84)

Best Fine Dining

Benu Fine dining meets DJ styling in ingenious remixes of Pacific Rim classics and the best ingredients in the West. (p64)

Frances Rustic Italian flavors with sun-drenched California ingredients and exquisite finesse. (p141)

Californios Roots cuisine celebrating California's sunny coastal flavors and the Mission's deep Latin American heritage. (p123)

Wako Sensational seafood *omakase* in a California beach-shack setting. (p173)

Best Farmers Markets

Ferry Plaza Farmers Market Star chefs, heirloom ingredients, and food trucks at weekends. (pictured; p55)

Mission Community Market Nonprofit, neighborhood-run market with 30 local vendors offering farm-fresh ingredients and artisan-food meals. (p121)

Castro Farmers Market Local produce and artisan foods at moderate prices, plus charmingly offbeat folk-music groups. (p145)

Bar Open

No matter what you're having, SF bars, cafes and clubs are here to oblige, with anything from California wines and Bay spirits to local roasts. Adventurous drinking is abetted by local bartenders, who've been making good on gold-rush saloon history with potent drinks in delicate vintage glasses. SF baristas take their micro-roasts seriously.

Bars & Breweries

Tonight you're gonna party like it's 1899: you'll recognize SF drink historians by their Old Tom gin selections and vintage tiki barware displays. Beer buffs are also well served: SF's first brewery (1849) was built before the city was, and beer has been a staple ever since. Meanwhile, wine bars and urban wineries are increasingly offering top-notch, small-production California wines by the glass or *alla spina* (on tap).

Cafes

When San Francisco couples break up, the thorniest issue is: who gets the cafe? San Franciscans are fiercely loyal to specific roasts and baristas – especially in the Mission, Hayes Valley and North Beach – and the majority of first internet dates meet on neutral coffee grounds. When using free cafe wi-fi, remember: order something every hour, deal with interruptions graciously and don't leave laptops unattended. Phone calls are many baristas' pet peeve but texting is fine.

Clubs

DJs set the tone at clubs in SF, where the right groove gets everyone on the dance floor – blending gay and straight in a giddy motion blur. Most clubs charge $10 to $25 at the door. For discounted admission, show up before 10pm or sign up to the club's online guest list (look for a VIP or RSVP link). Seating may be reserved for bottle service at high-end clubs. You'll usually only wait 15 minutes to get in anywhere.

BOB KREISEL / ALAMY ©

Best Bars

Comstock Saloon Vintage Wild West saloon with potent, period-perfect concoctions and dainty bar bites. (p86)

Pagan Idol Tiki to a T, with Hemingway-esque rum drinks served in skulls and volcano eruptions. (p67)

Trick Dog The ultimate theme bar switches up drinks and decor every few months to match SF obsessions: murals, horoscopes, conspiracy theories... (p125)

Best Cafes

Caffe Trieste Legendary North Beach cafe fueling epic Beat poetry and weekend accordion jams since the '50s. (pictured; p88)

Ritual Coffee Roasters Heady roasts, local art and sociable seating in a cult roastery-cafe. (p127)

Sightglass Coffee This SoMa roastery looks industrial but serves small-batch roasts from family farms. (p68)

Trouble Coffee Co Driftwood seating, espresso in stoneware and surfers hunched over coconuts. (p175)

Andytown Coffee Ocean Beach days demand Snowy Plover gelato and espresso combos. (p174)

Best Dance Clubs

EndUp Epic 24-hour dance sessions in an urban-legendary SoMa LGBTIQ+ club since 1973. (p67)

El Rio Get down in the Mission and flirt internationally in the backyard. (p126)

Club OMG Mixed-gender club where the clientele comes out to play. (p66)

Madrone Art Bar Nudge aside the art installations and clear the floor: it's a Prince/Michael dance-off. (p157)

Treasure Hunt

All those tricked-out dens, well-stocked spice racks and fabulous ensembles don't just pull themselves together – San Franciscans scour their city for them. Eclectic originality is SF's signature style, and that's not one-stop shopping. But consider the thrill of the hunt: while shopping, you can watch fish theater and trade fashion tips with professional drag queens.

CHAMELEONSEYE / SHUTTERSTOCK ©

Opening Hours

Most stores are open daily from 10am to 6pm or 7pm, though hours often run 11am to 8pm Saturday and 11am to 6pm Sunday. Stores in the Mission and the Haight tend to open later and keep erratic hours; many Downtown stores stay open until 8pm.

Sales Tax

Combined SF city and California state sales taxes tack 8.75% onto the price of your purchase. This tax is not refundable.

Adventures in Retail

Indie designers and vintage shops supply original style on SF's most boutique-studded streets: Haight (pictured), Divisadero, Valencia, Hayes, upper Grant, Fillmore, Union and Polk. For further adventures in alt-retail, don't miss **West Coast Craft** (http://westcoastcraft.com; Fort Mason Center; ⊙mid-Jun & mid-Nov) and **Art Market San Francisco** (http://artmarketsf.com; Fort Mason Center; ⊙last weekend Apr).

Best Shopping

City Lights Books If you can't find nirvana in the Poetry Chair upstairs, try Lost Continents in the basement. (p80)

826 Valencia Your friendly neighborhood pirate-supply store and publishing house; proceeds support on-site youth writing programs. (p118)

Bi-Rite SF's best-curated selection of local artisan chocolates, cured meats and small-production wines. (p132)

Park Life Art, books, Aesthetics team T-shirts and design objects make SF seem exceptionally gifted. (p175)

Apothecarium Wonderland of cannabis edibles to whet your California appetite. (p143)

Freebies

San Francisco may be one of the most spendy cities in America, but that doesn't mean a determined frugal traveler can't hunt down the occasional gratis museum, concert, snack, view or experience. Particularly in the summertime, you'll stumble on free events galore.

EDDIEHERNANDEZPHOTOGRAPHY / SHUTTERSTOCK ©

Fun at No Charge

See SF history in motion at the free Cable Car Museum (p94), or head to 24th St to see Balmy Alley murals and hang with skaters at Potrero del Sol/ La Raza Skatepark. Daredevils can conquer the concrete Seward Street slides (p141) in the Castro, while romantics can attend free lunchtime concerts at Old St Mary's and, in summer, at Yerba Buena Gardens (p62). Graze on free samples at the Ferry Building (p54), and score free trinkets in exchange for a bartered song, drawing or poem at 826 Valencia (p118).

Best Free Events

Amoeba Music concerts Rockers, DJs and hip-hop heroes give free shows in-store. (p160)

Giants baseball Catch a glimpse of the action and join the party at the Embarcadero waterfront promenade behind left field. (p70)

First Tuesdays Many SF museums are free the first Tuesday of the month, including the de Young. (p165)

Live Music

○ The West goes wild for free bluegrass at **Hardly Strictly Bluegrass** (pictured; www. hardlystrictlybluegrass.com; ☉Oct) in Golden Gate Park, with three days of concerts by 100-plus bands and seven stages of headliners.

○ Festival Free concerts at **Stern Grove** (www.sterngrove.org; ☉Jun-Aug), Golden Gate Park's natural amphitheater. Music ranges from Afrobeat jazz to SF Opera.

Under the Radar San Francisco

STEVE ESTVANIK / SHUTTERSTOCK ©

You may think you know San Francisco from social media – which was invented here, after all – but this town remains full of surprises. Technology too weird for smartphones floats on SF piers, and streets showcase art too radical for museums.

Best Street Art

Balmy Alley Since 1973, muralistas have transformed back-alley garage doors into beloved landmarks – from murals commemorating Frida Kahlo's 1930 San Francisco honeymoon to Lucía González Ippolito's *Women of the Resistance*. (p113)

Clarion Alley This collective-curated outdoor gallery showcases topical murals from Megan Wilson's *Tax the Rich* to Tanya Wischerath's portraits of SF's trailblazing transgender activists. (p115)

24th Street The Mission's Calle 24 Latino Cultural District features mural-covered Victorians, bodegas and bookstores from Mission Street to Potrero Avenue – nonprofit Precita Eyes (p113) covers highlights on muralist-led tours.

Haight Street The '60s counterculture epicenter maintains radical street cred with Anarchists of the Americas murals at Bound Together Anarchist Book Collective, Haight Ashbury Free Clinic's Healthcare Is a Right mural at 558 Clayton, and Joana Zegri's 1967 Evolution Rainbow mural at the corner of Cole and Haight. (p148)

Best Weird Tech

Exploratorium When sun illuminates the Golden Gate Bridge, Pier 15 remains mysteriously misty along Fujiko Nakawa's Fog Bridge – one of many mind-boggling exhibits by ingenious Exploratorium inventors. (p39)

Internet Archive (https://archive.org) Lost blogs, Betamax and Grateful Dead tapes are found in this temple-turned-mega-library. Over 30 years, volunteers here digitized 70 petabytes of data – including 616 billion web pages – for posterity, not profit.

Wave Organ Past the yacht club in the Marina district, eerie sounds wheeze from repurposed cemetery statues, reconfigured into sound-sculpture by artists Peter Richards and George Gonzalez.

Musée Mécanique Drop a coin into one of the Musée's 300+ vintage arcade games to start a Wild West saloon brawl, kick off can-can dances, or send Ms. Pacman on rampages. (pictured; p49)

Audium Since 1967, audiophiles have gathered in pitch dark to experience psychedelic "room compositions" emitted from 176 floor-to-ceiling speakers. (p106)

Museums & Galleries

CHRIS ALLAN / SHUTTERSTOCK ©

Most major museums are downtown, though Golden Gate Park is home to the de Young Museum and the California Academy of Sciences. Galleries are clustered downtown and in North Beach, the Mission, Potrero Flats and Dogpatch.

Best Museums

SFMOMA Expand horizons with cutting-edge contemporary collections in SF's super-sized art museum. (pictured; p56)

Exploratorium Totally trippy hands-on exhibits test scientific theories and blow minds at Pier 15. (p39)

de Young Museum Global art and craft masterworks showcase provocative ideas and enviable hand-eye coordination. (p165)

Asian Art Museum Sightsee halfway across the globe in an hour, from romantic Persian miniatures to daring Chinese installation art. (p61)

Legion of Honor Iconic impressionist paintings, 90,000 graphic artworks, and weekend organ recitals amid Rodin sculptures. (p170)

Best Galleries for Provocation

Catharine Clark Gallery (Potrero Hill) Art revolutions are instigated here. (p124)

Luggage Store Gallery (Civic Center) This plucky nonprofit gallery has brought signs of life to one of the Tenderloin's toughest blocks for two decades. (p60)

Yerba Buena Center for the Arts (SoMa) Rock stars would be jealous of art stars at YBCA openings. (p70)

Anglim Gilbert Gallery (Financial District & Dogpatch) Has a 30-year legacy of launching art movements, from Beat assemblage to Bay Area conceptualists. (p120)

Haight Street Art Center (The Haight) Dedicated to works on paper and San Francisco's signature art form: screen-printed posters. (p154)

Art is Everywhere

Art explodes from frames and jumps off the pedestal in San Francisco, where murals, street performances and impromptu sidewalk altars flow from alleyways right into galleries.

Active San Francisco

OOMKA / SHUTTERSTOCK ©

San Franciscans love the outdoors, and their historic conservation efforts have protected acres of parks, beaches and woodlands for all to enjoy. This city lives for sunny days spent biking, skating, surfing and drifting on the Bay. Foggy days are spent making art projects, but nights are for dancing and Giants games.

Fun in the Sun

On sunny weekends, SF is out admiring nature, jogging, kite-flying, golfing or cycling across the Golden Gate Bridge (pictured). Even on foggy days, don't neglect sunscreen: UV rays penetrate SF's thin cloud cover.

Crissy Field (p38) has a 2.5-mile jogging track, and trails run 3 miles through Golden Gate Park (p164) from the Panhandle to Ocean Beach. The Presidio (p38) offers ocean breezes through eucalyptus trees.

The San Francisco Bicycle Coalition (p181) produces the San Francisco Bike Map & Walking Guide, which outlines the Wiggle route and shows how to avoid traffic and hills. For further planning, put your smartphone to work finding the perfect route using the San Francisco Bike Route Planner (http://amarpai.com/bikemap).

Golfers tee up and enjoy mild weather, clipped greens and gorgeous views on SF's top public courses: **Lincoln Park**

Golf Course (www.sfrecpark.org) and **Golden Gate Municipal Golf Course** (☎415-751-8987; www.goldengateparkgolf.com).

Best for Activities

Golden Gate Park Lawn-bowling, skating and cycling – especially on car-free Sundays. (p164)

Stow Lake Glide across the lake by paddleboat. (p167)

Urban Putt Minigolf through SF landmarks. (p120)

Spinnaker Sailing Sail across the bay. (p40)

Crissy Field Kitesurfing with a Golden Gate Bridge backdrop. (p38)

For Kids

San Francisco has the fewest kids per capita of any US city and, according to SPCA data, 5000 to 35,000 more dogs than children live here. Yet many locals make a living entertaining kids – from Pixar animators to video-game designers – and this town is full of attractions for young people.

SABRINA DALBESIO / LONELY PLANET ©

Be Transported

When junior gearheads demand to know how cable cars work, the Cable Car Museum (p94) lets them glimpse the inner workings for themselves. Take a joyride on the Powell-Hyde cable car to Fisherman's Wharf, where you can enter submarine stealth mode aboard the USS Pampanito (p49) and climb aboard schooners and steamships at the Maritime National Historical Park (p49). Future sea captains will enjoy model-boat weekend regattas at Spreckels Lake in Golden Gate Park (p164).

Meet the Creatures

Penguins, buffalo and an albino alligator call Golden Gate Park (p164) home. Chase butterflies through the rainforest dome, pet starfish in the petting zoo and squeal in the Eel Forest at the California Academy of Sciences (p165). Get a whiff of insect breath from carnivorous flowers at the Conservatory of Flowers (p166) – pee-eeww! – and brave the shark tunnel at Aquarium of the Bay (p47). **San Francisco Zoo** (☏ 415-753-7080; www.sfzoo.org) is out of the way but worth the trip for monkeys, lemurs and giraffes.

Best Playgrounds

Golden Gate Park Swings, monkey bars, play castles with slides, hillside slides and a vintage carousel. (p164)

Dolores Park Jungle gym, Mayan pyramid and picnic tables. (p118)

Yerba Buena Gardens Grassy downtown playground surrounded by museums, cinemas and kid-friendly dining. (pictured; p62)

LGBTIQ+ San Francisco

It doesn't matter where you're from or who you love: if you're here and queer, welcome home. San Francisco is America's most LGBTIQ-friendly city, and though some call it the retirement home of the young – the sidewalks roll up early here – there's nowhere easier to be out and proud.

LGBTIQ+ Scene

The intersection of 18th and Castro (pictured) is the historic center of the gay world, but dancing queens and trans kids head to SoMa to mix it up at thump-thump clubs. Drag shows have been a nightlife staple here since the 1800s. Meanwhile, the women into women are busy sunning on the patio at **Wild Side West** (☎415-647-3099; www.wildsidewest. com; 424 Cortland Ave; ⏰2pm-2am; ▢24) or El Rio (p126), screening documentaries at the Roxie Cinema (p129), hitting happy hour at Jolene's (p126), inventing new technologies at SF women's/nonbinary hackerspaces, and raising kids in Noe Valley and Bernal Heights. The Mission remains the preferred 'hood of womxn, femmes, bois, dykes on bikes, trans female-to-males (FTMs) and nonbinary folx right across the rainbow spectrum. Gender need not apply in SF, where the DMV officially acknowledges trans-queer identities.

Best LGBTIQ+ Dance Parties

Aunt Charlie's Lounge (p66) Knock-down, drag-out winner for gender-bending shows and dance-floor freakiness in a tiny space.

El Rio (p126) Mix it up with world music, salsa, house, live bands and SF's flirtiest patio.

Stud (p66) Shows and DJs nightly, plus the tantalizing aroma of bourbon, cologne and testosterone.

Powerhouse (p66) DJs most nights, gogo dancers and strong drinks at the classic SoMa cruise bar.

EndUp (p67) Hit your groove Saturday night and work it until Monday.

BRIGITTE MERLE / GETTY IMAGES ©

Best LGBTIQ+ Daytime Hangouts

Dolores Park (p118) Sun and cityscapes on hillside 'Gay Beach,' plus political protests.

Baker Beach (p38) Only Baker Beach regulars know you can get goose bumps there.

El Rio (p126) Catch back-patio drag performances at Daytime Realness on Sundays.

Eagle Tavern (p66) The Sunday-afternoon beer busts cater to leather scenesters.

Best Places to Stay

Parker Guest House (☎415-621-3222, 888-520-7275; www.parkerguest house.com) Top choice for comfort and style.

Inn on Castro (☎415-861-0321; www.innoncastro. com) Vintage Victorian styled with disco-era furnishings.

Willows Inn (☎415-431-4770; www.willowssf.com) Best for budgeteers who don't mind sharing a bath.

Beck's Motor Lodge (☎415-621-8212; www.becksmotorlodge.com) Upgraded motel rooms in the heart of the Castro.

Inn San Francisco (☎800-359-0913, 415-641-0188; www.innsf.com) Swanky B&B in the heart of the Mission.

News & Events

The Bay Area Reporter (www.ebar.com) Released every Wednesday since 1971; news and events.

San Francisco Bay Times (http://sfbaytimes.com) News and calendar listings.

Gloss Magazine (www.glossmagazine.net) Nightlife and parties.

Four Perfect Days

Day 1

BJØRN BAKSTAD / SHUTTERSTOCK ©

Hike up to **Coit Tower** (pictured; p74) for 360-degree panoramas. Take the scenic **Filbert Street Steps** (p83) to the Embarcadero and wander across Fog Bridge, then check out the **Exploratorium** (p39).

Ferry to **Alcatraz** (p32), taking in **Golden Gate Bridge** (p34) views on the ride. Hop on the Powell-Mason cable car to North Beach and visit free-speech landmark **City Lights Books** (p80) and the **Beat Museum** (p80).

Cackle at the comics of **Cobb's Comedy Club** (p90) or razor-sharp satire at **Beach Blanket Babylon** (p89). Toast the wildest night in the west with potent pisco sours at **Comstock Saloon** (p86) or Chinese mai tais at **Li Po** (p86).

Day 2

TOMS AUZINS / SHUTTERSTOCK ©

Hop on the N Judah to **Golden Gate Park** (p164) to see carnivorous plants at the **Conservatory of Flowers** (p166) and Oceanic masks at the **de Young Museum** (p165). Explore the rainforest dome of the **California Academy of Sciences** (p165) before blissing out at the **Japanese Tea Garden** (pictured; p166).

Beachcomb **Ocean Beach** (p171) up to the **Beach Chalet** (p174) to glimpse 1930s frescoes. Follow the **Coastal Trail** (p170) past **Sutro Baths** (p170) and **Lands End** (p170) for **Golden Gate Bridge** (p34) vistas and priceless paper artworks at the **Legion of Honor** (p170).

Psychedelic posters and top acts make for rock-legendary nights at the **Fillmore** (p106).

Day 3

GG-FOTO / SHUTTERSTOCK ©

Hit pagoda-topped Grant St for an eye-opening **Red Blossom** (p86) tea tasting and an education at the **Chinese Historical Society of America** (p80). Wander temple-lined **Waverly Place** (p82) and find your fortune at **Golden Gate Fortune Cookies** (p91).

Take the Powell-Hyde cable car past zigzagging Lombard Street to the **Maritime National Historical Park** (p49). Save the world from Space Invaders at **Musée Mécanique** (p49) and watch sea lions cavort at **Pier 39** (pictured; p47).

Browse Hayes Valley boutiques before your concert at the **SF Symphony** (p68) or **SFJAZZ Center** (p158), and toast your good fortune at **Smuggler's Cove** (p157).

Day 4

ANTONIOGUT / SHUTTERSTOCK ©

Wander 24th St past mural-covered bodegas to **Balmy Alley** (p113), where the Mission *muralista* movement began in the 1970s. Pause for pirate supplies at **826 Valencia** (p118) and continue to San Francisco's first building, **Mission Dolores** (p119).

Spot Victorian 'Painted Ladies' around **Alamo Square** (p154) and stroll the tree-lined Panhandle to Stanyan. Window-shop your way down hippie-historic **Haight Street** (p148) past record stores and vintage emporiums.

Catch a show at the deco-fabulous **Castro Theatre** (pictured; p143). Club kids cruise over to **440 Castro** (p142), while straight-friendly crowds clink tiki drinks amid airplane wreckage at **Last Rites** (p141).

Need to Know

For detailed information, see Survival Guide p177

Currency
US dollar ($)

Language
English

Visas
USA Visa Waiver Program (VWP) allows nationals from 38 countries to enter the US without a visa.

Money
ATMs widely available; credit cards accepted at most hotels, stores and restaurants.

Cell Phones
Most US cell (mobile) phones besides the iPhone operate on CDMA, not the European standard GSM.

Time
Pacific Standard Time (GMT/UTC minus eight hours)

Tipping
At restaurants, add 15% to 25% to the bill. Count on $1 to $2 per drink at bars, $2 per bag to hotel porters, and 15% or $1 minimum per taxi ride.

Daily Budget

Budget: Less than $150
Dorm bed: $33–60
Food-truck fare: $5–15
Mission murals: free
Castro Theatre show: $12

Midrange: $150–350
Downtown hotel/home-share: $130–195
Ferry Building meal: $20–45
Symphony rush tickets: $25
Muni Passport: $29

Top End: More than $350
Boutique hotel: $195–390
Chef's tasting menu: $90–260
City Pass (Muni, cable cars plus four attractions): $94
Opera orchestra seats: $90–150

Advance Planning

Two months before Make reservations at Benu, build stamina for Coit Tower climbs and Mission bar crawls.

Three weeks before Book Alcatraz tour, Chinatown History Tour or Precita Eyes Mission Mural Tour.

One week before Search for tickets to the American Conservatory Theater, SF Symphony, SF Opera and Oasis drag shows.

Arriving in San Francisco

✈ San Francisco International Airport (SFO)

Fast rides to downtown SF on BART cost $9.65; ride-share $30 to $50; door-to-door shuttle $19 to $23; SamTrans express bus 398 to Transbay Terminal Center $2.50; or taxi $45 to $60.

✈ Oakland International Airport (OAK)

Catch BART from the airport to downtown SF ($10.95); take a shared shuttle for $35 to $45; or pay $40 to $80 for a ride-share or taxi to SF destinations.

🚃 Emeryville Amtrak Station

Located outside Oakland, this depot serves West Coast and nationwide train routes; Amtrak runs free shuttles to/from San Francisco.

Getting Around

San Franciscans mostly walk, bike, ride Muni or ride-share instead of taking a car or cab.

🚃 Cable Cars

Frequent, slow and scenic, from 6am to 12:30am daily. Single rides cost $7; for frequent use, get a Muni Passport ($23 per day).

🚌 Muni Streetcar and Bus

Reasonably fast, but schedules vary by line; infrequent after 9pm. Fares are $2.75 cash, or $2.50 with a reloadable Clipper card.

🚊 BART

High-speed transit to East Bay, Mission St, SF airport and Millbrae, where it connects with Caltrain.

🚕 Taxi

Fares are about $3 per mile; meters start at $3.50.

San Francisco Neighborhoods

Golden Gate Bridge & the Marina (p31)
In full view of San Francisco's iconic landmark, you'll find Yoda (in statue form), nature and nudity.

Japantown, Fillmore & Pacific Heights (p99)
Remnants of cultural and ethnic diversity interwoven with quaint Victorians and upscale boutiques.

Golden Gate Bridge

Golden Gate Park

Haight Street

Golden Gate Park & the Avenues (p163)
SF's Wild West is where the bison roam, penguins waddle, hippies drum and surfers rip.

The Castro (p135)
Vibrant and proud, with the fabulous art deco theater, LGBTIQ+ rights history and rainbow crosswalks to prove it.

North Beach & Chinatown (p73)
Dragon gates and dim sum on one end of Grant St, parrots and espresso on the other – and poetry in every alley.

Downtown, Civic Center & SoMa (p53)
Flagship stores and museum shows by day, underground clubs and Bay Bridge lights by night.

Alcatraz

Fisherman's Wharf & the Piers

Russian Hill

Coit Tower

Cable Car Museum

Ferry Building

Nob Hill

San Francisco Museum of Modern Art

The Haight & Hayes Valley (p147)
Sixties flashbacks, radical fashion, free music and pricey skateboards.

Mission Murals

The Mission (p111)
A book in one hand, a burrito in the other, murals all around.

San Francisco International
(8.5mi)

Explore
San Francisco

San Francisco's Walking Tours

Explore ◈
Golden Gate Bridge & the Marina

Mostly built in the 1930s atop 1906 earthquake debris, this swanky waterfront neighborhood overlooks the Golden Gate Bridge and Alcatraz. It offers chic boutiques and restaurants in a former cow pasture, along with food trucks in a former military depot.

The Short List

○ **Golden Gate Bridge (p34)** *Strolling across just after the fog clears, revealing magnificent views of downtown San Francisco with sailboats plying the waves below.*

○ **Alcatraz (p32)** *Feeling cold winds blow as you imagine the misery of prison life – not to mention the ingenuity required for an escape.*

○ **Exploratorium (p39)** *Letting your curiosity run amok in this hands-on museum of science, art and human perception. Don't miss the Tactile Dome.*

○ **Crissy Field (p38)** *Frolicking in a waterfront nature preserve and enjoying a picnic lunch with superb Golden Gate views.*

Getting There & Around

🚌 Major routes to the Marina from downtown include the 47 and 49. The free PresidiGo shuttle is based at the Presidio Transit Center and loops the Presidio.

🚗 There's parking at Fort Mason, Crissy Field and the Presidio.

Neighborhood Map on p36

Golden Gate Bridge (p34) MICHAEL LAWENKO DELA PAZ / GETTY IMAGES ©

Top Experience 📷
Escape to Alcatraz

Alcatraz: for over 150 years, the name has given the innocent chills and the guilty cold sweats. Over the decades it's been a military prison, a forbidding maximum-security penitentiary and disputed territory between Native American activists and the FBI. So it's no surprise that the first step you take onto 'the Rock' seems to cue ominous music: dunh-dunh-dunnnnh!

◎ MAP P36, H1

📞 Alcatraz Cruises
415-981-7625

www.alcatrazcruises.com

tours adult/child 5-11 day $39/25, night $47/28

🕐 call center 8am-7pm, ferries depart Pier 33 half-hourly 8:45am-3:50pm, night tours 5:55pm & 6:30pm

Early History

It all started innocently enough back in 1775, when Spanish lieutenant Juan Manuel de Ayala sailed the San Carlos past the 22-acre island that he called Isla de los Alcatraces (Isle of the Pelicans). In 1859 a new post on Alcatraz became the first US West Coast fort and it soon proved handy as a holding pen for Civil War deserters, insubordinates and the court-martialed. By 1902 the four cell blocks of wooden cages were rotting and unsanitary. The army began building a new concrete military prison in 1909, but upkeep was expensive and the US soon had other things to worry about: WWI, financial ruin and flappers.

Prison Life

In 1922, when the 18th Amendment to the Constitution declared selling liquor a crime, rebellious Jazz Agers weren't prepared to give up their tipple – and gangsters kept the booze coming. Authorities were determined to make a public example of criminal ringleaders and in 1934 the Federal Bureau of Prisons took over Alcatraz as a prominent showcase for its crime-fighting efforts. The Rock averaged only 264 inmates, but its roster read like a list of America's Most Wanted. A-list criminals doing time on Alcatraz included Chicago crime boss Al 'Scarface' Capone, dapper kidnapper George 'Machine Gun' Kelly, hot-headed Harlem ma-fioso and sometime poet 'Bumpy' Johnson, and Morton Sobell, the military contractor found guilty of Soviet espionage along with Julius and Ethel Rosenberg.

Today, first-person accounts of daily life in the Alcatraz lockup are included on the excellent self-guided audio tour. But take your headphones off for just a moment and you'll notice the sound of carefree city life traveling from across the water: this is the torment that made perilous escapes into riptides worth the risk.

★ Top Tips

○ Book well ahead: a month for self-guided daytime visits, two to three months for popular nighttime tours.

○ The weather changes fast and it's often windy and much colder on Alcatraz, so wear extra layers, long pants and a cap.

○ When visiting by day, to avoid crowds book the day's first or last boat. You need only reserve the outbound boat, not the return, so take your time.

✕ Take a Break

Most people spend three to four hours; bring lunch to linger longer. Note: eating is allowed only at the ferry dock. There's limited food on the island, only bottled water, coffee and nuts.

Top Experience
Marvel at the Golden Gate Bridge

The city's most spectacular icon, a suspension bridge painted in the signature shade called International Orange, towers 80 stories above the roiling waters of the Golden Gate. Joseph B Strauss was the engineering mastermind behind the marvel, but architects Gertrude and Irving Murrow and daredevil laborers also deserve credit.

◉ MAP P36, A1

☏ toll information
877-229-8655

www.goldengatebridge.org

Hwy 101

northbound free, southbound $7-8

🚌 28, all Golden Gate Transit buses

Building the Bridge

Not until the early 1920s did the City of San Francisco seriously investigate building a bridge over the treacherous, windblown strait. The War Department owned the land on both sides and pushed for a functional bridge; safe and solid. Instead, a green light was given to the counter-proposal by Strauss and the Murrows for a subtle suspension span that harmonized with the natural environment. Laborers dove into the treacherous riptides of the bay and got the bridge under way in 1933. Four years later they completed the world's longest suspension bridge – nearly 2 miles long, with 746ft suspension towers, higher than any construction west of New York.

Vista Points

San Franciscans have passionate perspectives on every subject, especially their signature landmark. As far as best views go, cinema buffs believe Hitchcock had it right: seen from below at **Fort Point** (☏ 415-504-2334; www.nps.gov/fopo; Marine Dr; admission free; ⏱ 10am-5pm Fri-Sun; P ; 🚌 28) the 1937 bridge induces a thrilling case of vertigo. Fog aficionados prefer the north-end lookout at Marin's Vista Point, to watch gusts billow through bridge cables like dry ice at a Kiss concert.

Bridge Crossings

To see both sides of the Golden Gate debate, hike or bike the 1.7-mile span. Pedestrians take the eastern sidewalk, beginning from the parking area off Lincoln Blvd. If 3.4 miles round-trip seems too much, take a bus to the north side then walk back. By bicycle, from the toll-plaza parking area ride toward the Roundhouse, then follow signs to the western sidewalk, reserved for bikes only.

★ Top Tips

○ City Guides offers free tours of the bridge (www.sfcityguides.org), departing Sunday and Thursday at 11am, from the statue of Joseph Strauss by the visitor center on the bridge's SF side.

○ Dress warmly before crossing the bridge on foot or bike, with a water-resistant outer layer to break the wind and fog.

○ For on-site information, stop into the Bridge Pavilion Visitor Center.

✕ Take a Break

You'll find refreshments only at the SF end of the bridge by the Bridge Pavilion. Otherwise, there's nothing nearby for food or drink.

Golden Gate Bridge & the Marina Marvel at the Golden Gate Bridge

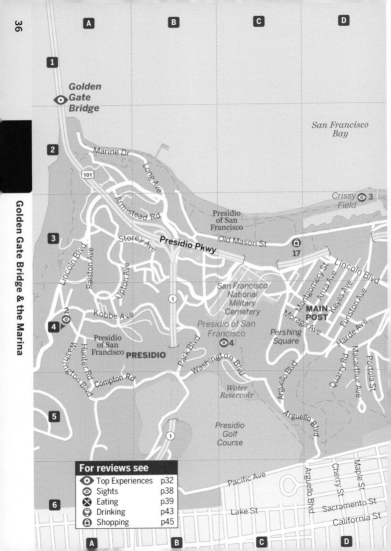

A **B** **C** **D**

1

Golden
Gate
Bridge

San Francisco
Bay

2

Marine Dr

Long Ave

101

Crissy 3
Field

Armistead Rd

Presidio
of San
Francisco

Old Mason St

17

3

Storey Ave

Presidio Pkwy

Lincoln Blvd

Ralston Ave

Upton Ave

Lincoln Blvd

Montgomery St

Anza Ave

Keyes Ave

Funston Ave

MAIN
POST

Moraga Ave

Macarthur Ave

Harde Ave

Portola St

San Francisco
National
Military
Cemetery

Presidio of San
Francisco 4

1

Pershing
Square

4

Kobbe Ave

Hunter Rd

Washington Blvd

Presidio
of San
Francisco **PRESIDIO**

Park Blvd

Washington Blvd

Arguello Blvd

Quarry Rd

Compton Rd

Water
Reservoir

Arguello Blvd

5

1

Presidio
Golf
Course

Arguello Blvd

Cherry St

Maple St

For reviews see

⊙	Top Experiences	p32
⊙	Sights	p38
⊗	Eating	p39
🍷	Drinking	p43
🛍	Shopping	p45

Pacific Ave

Lake St

Sacramento St

California St

6

A **B** **C** **D**

E **F** **G** **H**

Alcatraz **1**

2

Marina
Green
Yacht Rd
Marina Green Dr
Fort Mason
Center

9 **1**
12 **16**
Off
the
Grid
Fort
Mason

13

Yacht
Harbor
Oceanic Society
Expeditions
Marina Blvd
Jefferson St
Beach St
Cervantes Blvd
Fillmore St
Beach St
Laguna St
Bay St

Mason St
Palace
of Fine
Arts
North Point St
Baker St
Avila St
Pierce St
Bay St
George R Moscone
Recreation Center
Francisco St
Chestnut St **3**

101
Palace Dr
5
Bay St
Francisco St

Gorgas Ave
Richardson Ave
11 Chestnut St
Lombard St
Kennedy Ave
Presidio
of San
Francisco
Lombard St

Greenwich St **10**
COW
HOLLOW
Octavia St
8

4

Filbert St
Union St **14**
15
Webster St
Buchanan St
6
7
Laguna St

Presidio Blvd
Broderick St
Divisadero St
Green St
Vallejo St

Clarke St
Presidio Blvd
Lyon Steps
Baker St
Lyon St
Scott St
Pierce St
Steiner St
Broadway
Pacific Ave
Jackson St
Washington St
5

Broadway
Pacific Ave
**PACIFIC
HEIGHTS**
Alta
Plaza
Park
University
of the
Pacific

Pacific Ave
Jackson St
Washington St
Clay St
Presidio Ave
Lyon St
Baker St
Broderick St
Clay St
Sacramento St
Fillmore St
California St
Pine St

Pine St **6**

Mayfair Dr
Pine St
Bush St
N 0 500 m
0 0.25 miles

E **F** **G** **H**

Sights

Fort Mason Center

AREA

1 ⊙ MAP P36, H2

San Francisco takes subversive glee in turning military installations into venues for nature, fine dining and out-there experimental art. Evidence: Fort Mason, once a shipyard and embarkation point for WWII troops, now a vast cultural center and gathering place for events, drinking and eating. Wander the waterfront, keeping your eyes peeled for fascinating outdoor art-and-science installations designed by the Exploratorium. (☏415-345-7500; www.fortmason.org; cnr Marina Blvd & Laguna St; P; ☐22, 28, 30, 43, 47, 49)

Baker Beach

BEACH

2 ⊙ MAP P36, A4

Picnic amid wind-sculpted pines, fish from craggy rocks or frolic nude at mile-long Baker Beach, with spectacular views of the Golden Gate. Crowds come weekends, especially on fog-free days; arrive early. For nude sunbathing among straight women and gay men, head to the north. Families in clothing stick to the south, nearer parking. Mind the currents and the c-c-cold water. (☏10am-5pm 415-561-4323; www.nps.gov/prsf; ⊙sunrise-sunset; P; ☐29, PresidiGo Shuttle)

Crissy Field

PARK

3 ⊙ MAP P36, D3

War is for the birds at Crissy Field, a military airstrip turned waterfront nature preserve with knockout Golden Gate views. Where military aircraft once zoomed in for landings, bird-watchers now huddle in the silent rushes of a reclaimed tidal marsh. Joggers pound beachside trails and the only security alerts are raised by puppies suspiciously sniffing surfers. On foggy days, stop by the certified-green **Warming Hut** (☏415-561-3042; www.parksconservancy.org/visit/eat/warming-hut.html) to browse regional nature books and warm up with fairtrade coffee. (☏415-561-4700; www.nps.gov; 1199 East Beach; ☐30, PresidiGo Shuttle)

Presidio of San Francisco

PARK

4 ⊙ MAP P36, C4

Explore that splotch of green on the map between Baker Beach and Crissy Field and you'll find parade grounds, Yoda, a centuries-old adobe wall and some fascinating art projects. What started as a Spanish fort built by Ohlone conscripts in 1776 is now a treasure hunt of surprises. Begin your adventures at the Main Post to get trail maps at the **visitor center** (www.presidio.gov; 210 Lincoln Blvd; ⊙10am-5pm; ☐PresidiGo Shuttle) and inquire about site-specific art installations by Andy Goldsworthy. (📞415-561-4323; www.nps.gov/prsf; 🕑dawn-dusk; P; 🚌28, 43)

Palace of Fine Arts   MONUMENT

5 ◉ MAP P36, E3

Like a fossilized party favor, this romantic, ersatz Greco-Roman ruin is the city's memento from the 1915 Panama-Pacific International Exposition. The original, designed by celebrated Berkeley architect Bernard Maybeck, was of wood, burlap and plaster, then later reinforced. By the 1960s it was crumbling. The structure was recast in concrete so that future generations could gaze at the rotunda relief to glimpse 'Art under attack by materialists, with idealists leaping to her rescue.' A glorious spot to wander day or night. (📞510-599-4651; www.lovethepalace.org; Palace Dr; admission free; 🕑24hr; 🚌28, 30, 43)

Eating

Gio Gelati   GELATO $

6 🍴 MAP P36, H4

Gelato chef Patrizia Pasqualetti was well-known in Italy for her family's gelato shop, and here in SF she's re-creating those tried-and-true flavors, only with local fruit, dairy and

Science & Art

Is there a science to skateboarding? Do toilets really flush counterclockwise in Australia? Combining science with art, San Francisco's dazzling hands-on **Exploratorium** (📞415-528-4444; www.exploratorium.edu; Pier 15/17; adult/child $30/20, 6-10pm Thu $20; 🕑10am-5pm Tue-Sun, over 18yr only 6-10pm Thu; P♿; Ⓜ︎E, F) nudges you to question how you know what you know. As thrilling as the exhibits is the setting: a 9-acre, glass-walled pier jutting over San Francisco Bay, with vast outdoor portions you can explore for free.

Covering 330,000 sq ft of indoor-outdoor space, the 600-plus exhibits have buttons to push, cranks to ratchet and dials to adjust, all made by artists and scientists at the in-house building shop. Try a punk hairdo, courtesy of the static-electricity station. Turn your body into the gnomon of a sundial. Slide, climb and feel your way – in total darkness – through the labyrinth of the **Tactile Dome** (Pier 15; admission day/after dark $15/10).

In 2013 the Exploratorium moved to its purpose-built solar-powered space, constructed in concert with scientific agencies, including the National Oceanic and Atmospheric Administration (NOAA), which hardwired the pier with sensors delivering real-time data on weather, wind, tides and the bay.

The Bay by Boat

Some of the best views of San Francisco are from the water – if the weather's fair, be sure to take a boat ride. At the time of research, the aim was to have every ferry and tour boat in the bay running on renewable diesel fuel made of fat, vegetable oils and grease in the near future. Following is a list of operators that will get you out on the bay.

Bay Cruises

Red & White Fleet (☎ 415-673-2900; www.redandwhite.com; Pier 43½; adult/child $34/25; ⬥; 🚻 47, Ⓜ E, F) operates multiple trips from Pier 43½; **Blue & Gold Fleet** (☎ 415-705-8200; www.blueandgoldfleet.com; Pier 41; adult/child 60min ferry tour $34/23, 30min high-speed boat ride $30/21; ⏱ 9am-6:30pm, varies seasonally; ⬥; 🚻 47, Ⓜ E, F) operates from Pier 41 and also offers 30-minute trips aboard its high-speed *Rocketboat*.

Sailboat Tours

If you prefer sailboats to ferries, hit the bay aboard the **Adventure Cat** (☎ 415-777-1630; www.adventurecat.com; Pier 39, Dock J; adult/child $45/25, sunset cruise $60; ⬥; 🚻 47, Ⓜ E, F) – a catamaran with a trampoline between its hulls – for a 90-minute bay cruise or sunset sail. Or charter a private sailboat, with or without skipper, from **Spinnaker Sailing** (☎ 415-543-7333; www.spinnaker-sailing.com; Pier 40, South Beach Harbor; skippered charters from $455, lessons from $105 per/hr; ⏱ 10am-5pm; 🚻 30, 45, Ⓜ N, T).

Paddle Tours

Explore the bay's calm eastern shoreline in a canoe or kayak from **City Kayak** (☎ 888-966-0953, 415-294-1050; www.citykayak.com; Pier 40, South Beach Harbor; kayak rentals per hour $35-125, lesson & rental $54, tours $54-89; ⏱ rentals noon-3pm, return by 5pm Thu-Mon; 🚻 30, 45, Ⓜ N, T), which guides tours and rents boats.

Whale-Watching Tours

To go beyond the Golden Gate and on to the open ocean, take one of the excellent trips operated by the **Oceanic Society** (Map p36, F3; ☎ 415-256-9604; www.oceanicsociety.org; 3950 Scott St; whale-watching trips per person $135; ⏱ office 9am-5pm Mon-Fri; 🚻 30).

nuts. The results are pure creamy deliciousness, and favorites among the 30 flavors include sour cherry crunch and the Portuguese milk with caramelized figs. (📞415-867-1306; www.giogelati.com; 1998 Union St; gelato from $4.50; 🕙10am-10pm Sun-Thu, to 11pm Fri & Sat; 🚌22, 41, 45)

Vegan Picnic
VEGAN $

7 🍴 MAP P36, H4

This place really nails its meat flavors, with vegan meatballs, faux crispy chicken sandwiches and imitation salami subs. Staff members couldn't be nicer and you'll especially think so when they present you with free, lip-smackin' samples. Breakfast is served all day, but heads up: some items (ahem, we're talking about you chicken and waffles) come

drowning in a mysterious, maple-y, mustard-y sauce. (📞415-323-3043; www.veganpicnic.com; 1977a Union St; mains $7-14; 🕙8am-6:30pm Mon-Fri, from 9am Sat & Sun; 🍴; 🚌22, 41, 45)

Kaiyo
FUSION $$

8 🍴 MAP P36, H4

For a deliciously deep dive into the cuisine of the Japanese-Peruvian diaspora, head to one of Cow Hollow's most playful and inventive restaurants, where the Pisco and whiskey cocktails are named for anime characters and a neon-green moss wall runs the length of the *izakaya*-style dining room. But the real adventure is the food. (📞415-525-4804; www.kaiyosf.com; 1838 Union St; small plates $12-28, share plates $19-28; 🕙5-10pm Tue-Thu, 4-11pm Fri, from 10:30am Sat & Sun; 🚌41, 45)

Red & White Fleet ferry

PLUMPZA / SHUTTERSTOCK ©

Golden Gate Bridge & the Marina Eating

Off the Grid Food Trucks

Spring through fall, some 30 **food trucks** (Map p36, H2; 📞415-339-5888; www.offthegrid.com; 2 Marina Blvd, Fort Mason Center; items $6-15; ⏱5-10pm Fri Mar-Oct; 👪; 🚌22, 28) and pop-up cubes circle their wagons at SF's largest mobile-gourmet hootenannies on Friday night at Fort Mason Center, and 11am to 4pm Sunday for Picnic at the Presidio on the Main Post lawn. These weekly parties are a great way to appreciate the breadth of the SF food scene while rubbing elbows with locals. Beer, wine and cocktails warm you up for dancing to live music and DJs.

Greens VEGETARIAN, CALIFORNIAN $$

9 🍴 MAP P36, H2

Career carnivores won't realize there's zero meat in the hearty black-bean chili, or in Greens' other flavor-packed vegetarian dishes, made using ingredients from a Zen farm in Marin. And, oh, what views! The Golden Gate rises just outside the window-lined dining room. The on-site cafe serves to-go lunches, but for sit-down meals, including Saturday and Sunday brunch, reservations are recommended. (📞415-771-6222; www.greensrestaurant.com; 2 Marina Blvd, Bldg A, Fort Mason Center; mains $18-28; ⏱5:30-9pm Mon, 11:30am-2:30pm & 5:30-9pm Tue-Fri; 10:30am-2:30pm & 5-9pm Sat & Sun; 📷👪; 🚌22, 28, 30, 43, 47, 49)

Atelier Crenn FRENCH $$$

10 🍴 MAP P36, G4

The menu arrives in the form of a poem and then come the signature white chocolate spheres filled with a burst of apple cider. If this seems an unlikely start to a meal, just wait for the geoduck rice tart in a glass dome frosted by liquid nitrogen, and about a dozen more plates inspired by the childhood of chef Dominique Crenn in Brittany, France. (📞415-440-0460; www.ateliercrenn.com; 3127 Fillmore St; tasting menu $335; ⏱5-9pm Tue-Sat; 🚌22, 28, 30, 43)

A16 ITALIAN $$$

11 🍴 MAP P36, F4

Even before A16 won a James Beard Award, it was hard to book, but persevere: the house-made mozzarella *burrata*, blister-crusted pizzas from the wood-burning oven and 15-page Italian wine list make it worth your while. Skip the spotty desserts and instead double up on adventurous appetizers. (📞415-771-2216; www.a16sf.com; 2355 Chestnut St; pizzas $18-22, mains $18-38; ⏱lunch 11:30am-2:30pm Fri-Sun, dinner 5:30-10pm Mon-Thu, 5:30-11pm Fri & Sat, 5-10pm Sun; 🚌28, 30, 43)

Drinking

Interval Bar & Cafe BAR

12 MAP P36, H2

Designed to stimulate discussion of philosophy and art, the Interval is a favorite spot in the Marina for cocktails and conversation. It's inside the Long Now Foundation, with floor-to-ceiling bookshelves, which contain the canon of Western lit, rising above the prototype of a 10,000-year clock – a fitting backdrop for a daiquiri, aged Tom Collins, or single-origin coffee, tea and snacks. (415-496-9187; www.theinterval.org; 2 Marina Blvd, Bldg A, Fort Mason Center; 10am-midnight; 10, 22, 28, 30, 47, 49)

Buena Vista Cafe BAR

13 MAP P36, H3

Warm your cockles with a prim little goblet of bitter-creamy Irish coffee, introduced to America at this destination bar that once served sailors and cannery workers. That old Victorian floor manages to hold up carousers and families alike, served community-style at round tables overlooking the cable-car turnaround at Victoria Park. (415-474-5044; www.thebuenavista.com; 2765 Hyde St; 9am-2am Mon-Fri, 8am-2am Sat & Sun; ; 30, 45, 47, Powell-Hyde)

Irish Coffees, Buena Vista Cafe

SVETLANASF / SHUTTERSTOCK ©

Marijuana Legalization

ⓘ

Congratulations: you're right on time for SF's latest tech boom, art show, green initiative, civil rights movement and (fair warning) marriage proposal. San Francisco has its ups and downs, but as anyone who's clung on to the side of a cable car will tell you, this town gives you one hell of a ride.

It should come as no surprise then that California voters passed a law legalizing marijuana for recreational and medical use starting in 2018. And actually, legalization activists first got organized in San Francisco in 1964, though the movement didn't get much press until San Francisco's Summer of Love in 1967, when police raided a crash pad on 710 Ashbury St – home to the Grateful Dead rock band. Eleven members of the household were arrested for possession of marijuana.

The raid backfired. The Grateful Dead quickly posted bail and held a press conference. Rather than protesting their innocence, they demanded the decriminalization of marijuana claiming that the dangers of pot were exaggerated. And besides, if everyone who used pot in San Francisco were arrested, the city would be empty.

The case made headlines, and with rock-star backing, the legalization movement took off. California put decriminalization to a vote in 1972, but it didn't pass. The issue became urgent during the AIDS crisis, when caregivers found that terminal patients' pain and wasting could be alleviated by medical marijuana use. In 1996, California's Compassionate Care Act made California the first US state allowing patients access to marijuana by prescription.

Today, California's legalization of pot for recreational and medical use enables the state to tax, license and monitor an industry that's been (ahem) budding for decades. For your own safety, avoid street dealers, who may adulterate their pot. Reputable, trailblazing, licensed cannabis dispensaries are available citywide, and many deliver through reliable, fast, tamper-proof delivery services such as HelloMD (www.hellomd.com).

You must be 18 plus with ID to buy pot, and you're expected to consume it responsibly in private spaces. Stay safe, and as the Grateful Dead would say: 'if you get confused, just let the music play.'

Radhaus

BEER HALL

It always feels like Octoberfest at this gleaming, Bavarian-style beer hall, installed in Fort Mason (see 1 Map p36, H2) in 2018. Offerings include nine taps of German beer, along with wine, kombucha and cider, to be paired with all the brats, currywurst, weisswurst and chicken schnitzel you can stomach. (415-445-4556; www.radhaussf.com; 2 Marina Blvd, Bldg A, Fort Mason Center; 11am-10pm; 10, 22, 28, 30, 47, 49)

Shopping

Sui Generis IIIa

CLOTHING

14 MAP P36, G4

Sui generis is Latin for 'one of a kind' – which is what you'll find at this high-end designer consignment shop that features recent seasons' looks, one-of-a-kind gowns and a few archival pieces by key couturiers from decades past. No jeans, no pants – unless they're leather or superglam. Yes, it's pricey, but far cheaper than you'd pay shopping retail. (415-800-7584; www.suigenerisconsignment. com; 2147 Union St; 11am-7pm Mon-Sat, to 5pm Sun; 22, 41, 45)

ATYS

HOMEWARES

15 MAP P36, G4

Tucked in a courtyard, this design showcase is like a museum store for exceptional, artistic household items – to wit, a mirrored coat rack, a rechargeable flashlight that turns a wineglass into a lamp, and a zero-emissions, solar-powered toy airplane. Expect sleek, modern designs of superior quality that you won't find anywhere else. (415-441-9220; www.atysdesign. com; 2149b Union St; 11am-6:30pm Mon-Sat, noon-6pm Sun; 22, 41, 45)

Flax Art & Design

DESIGN

16 MAP P36, H2

The city's finest art-supply store carries a dizzying array of ink, paints, pigment, brushes, frames, pens, pencils, markers and glues, plus paper in myriad varieties, from stationery and wrapping to drawing pads and sketch tablets. If you're a serious designer or artist, Flax is a must-visit. (415-530-3510; www.flaxart.com; 2 Marina Blvd, Bldg D, Fort Mason Center; 10am-6:30pm Mon-Sat, to 6pm Sun; 22, 28, 30, 43)

Sports Basement

SPORTS & OUTDOORS

17 MAP P36, C3

Specializing in odd lots of sporting goods at closeout prices, this 80,000-sq-ft sports-and-camping emporium is also the best place to rent wet suits for swims at Aquatic Park, gear for last-minute trips to Yosemite, or bikes to cross the nearby Golden Gate Bridge – and free parking makes it easy to trade your rental car for a bike. (415-934-2900; www.sportsbasement. com; 610 Old Mason St; 9am-9pm Mon-Fri, 8am-8pm Sat & Sun; 30, 43, PresidiGo Shuttle)

Top Experience
Take in the Sea Air at Fisherman's Wharf & the Piers

You won't find many fishermen at Fisherman's Wharf – though some still moor here, they're difficult to spot beyond the blinking neon and side-by-side souvenir shops. The Wharf may not be the 'real San Francisco,' but it holds a few surprises. Stick near the waterfront, where sea lions bray, street performers alarm unsuspecting passersby, and an aquarium and carousel entice kids.

www.fishermanswharf.org

admission free

🚼

🚌 19, 30, 47, 49,
🚋 Powell-Mason, Powell-Hyde, Ⓜ F

Pier 39

The focal point of Fisherman's Wharf isn't the waning fishing fleet but the carousel, carnival-like attractions, shops and restaurants of **Pier 39** (☎415-705-5500; www.pier39.com; cnr Beach St & the Embarcadero; P ♿; ☐47, 🚋Powell-Mason, Ⓜ E, F). Developed in the 1970s to revitalize tourism, the pier draws thousands of tourists daily, but it's really just a big outdoor shopping mall. On the plus side, its visitor center rents strollers, stores luggage and has free phone-charging stations.

By far the best reason to walk the pier is to spot the famous **sea lions**, who took over this coveted waterfront real estate in 1989. These unkempt squatters have been making a public display ever since and now they're San Francisco's favorite mascots. The valuable boat slips accommodate as many as 1000 sea lions that 'haul out' onto the docks between January and July. Follow signs along the pier's western edge – you can't miss 'em.

Aquarium of the Bay

Sharks circle overhead, manta rays sweep by and seaweed sways all around at the **Aquarium of the Bay** (☎415-623-5300; www.aquariumof thebay.org; adult/child/family $28/18/75; ⏱10am-8pm late May-early Sep, shorter hours rest of year; ♿; ☐47, 🚋Powell-Mason, Ⓜ E, F), where you wander through glass tubes surrounded by sea life from San Francisco Bay. Not for the claustrophobic, perhaps, but the thrilling fish-eye view leaves kids and parents amazed. Kids love the critters and touch pools upstairs, and the virtual reality theater.

San Francisco Carousel

A chariot awaits to whisk you and the kids past the Golden Gate Bridge, Alcatraz and other SF landmarks hand-painted onto this Italian **carousel** (1 ride $5, 3 rides $10; ⏱10am-9pm Sun-Thu, to 10pm Fri & Sat; ♿), pictured left, twinkling with 1800 lights, at the bayside end of Pier 39.

★ Top Tip

○ The Wharf is the only place in San Francisco where you won't see many San Franciscans. Once you've explored tall ships, consulted mechanical fortune tellers and eaten the obligatory clam chowder in a sourdough-bread bowl, hightail it away to more authentic neighborhoods, where you will discover the real soul of the city.

✕ Take a Break

Pick up a can of soda from one of the many souvenir shops, and catch your breath with a glorious bay view. Because there are so many tourist joints, the best place to take a break is not at a cafe or restaurant but on one of the numerous benches lining the waterfront. Alternatively, find the beach at Aquatic Park.

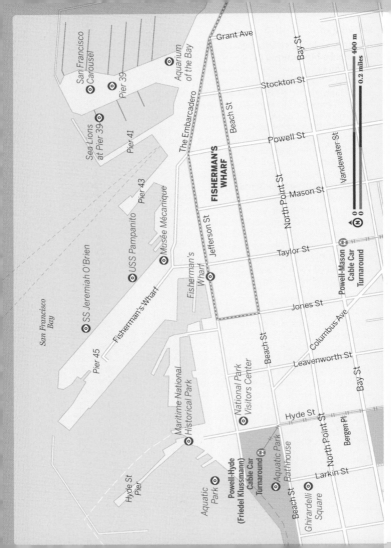

San Francisco Carousel

Pier 39

Aquarium of the Bay

Grant Ave

Bay St

Stockton St

Sea Lions at Pier 39

Pier 41

The Embarcadero

Beach St

Powell St

Pier 43

North Point St

Mason St

Vandewater St

FISHERMAN'S WHARF

Musée Mécanique

USS Pampanito

Jefferson St

Taylor St

Fisherman's Wharf

SS Jeremiah O'Brien

Fisherman's Wharf

San Francisco Bay

Jones St

Columbus Ave

Pier 45

Beach St

Leavenworth St

Powell-Mason Cable Car Turnaround

Bay St

Maritime National Historical Park

National Park Visitors Center

Hyde St

North Point St

Bergen Pl

Hyde St Pier

Powell-Hyde (Friedel Klussmann) Cable Car Turnaround

Aquatic Park Bathhouse

Larkin St

Aquatic Park

Beach St

North Point St

Ghirardelli Square

Aquatic Park

400 m

0.2 miles

Musée Mécanique

A flashback to penny arcades, the **Musée Mécanique** (📞 415-346-2000; www.museemecanique. com; Pier 45, Shed A; ⏰ 10am-8pm; 👶; 🚌 47, 🚃 Powell-Mason, Powell-Hyde, Ⓜ E, F) houses a mind-blowing collection of vintage mechanical amusements. Sinister, freckle-faced Laughing Sal has freaked out kids for over a century, but don't let this manic mannequin deter you from the best arcade west of Coney Island. A quarter lets you start brawls in Wild West saloons, peep at belly dancers through a vintage Mutoscope and even learn a cautionary tale about smoking opium.

Maritime National Historical Park

Five historic ships are floating museums at this **maritime national park** (📞 415-447-5000; www.nps.gov/safr; 499 Jefferson St, Hyde St Pier; 7-day ticket adult/child $15/free; ⏰ 9:30am-5pm Oct-May, to 5:30pm Jun-Sep; 👶; 🚌 19, 30, 47, 🚃 Powell-Hyde, Ⓜ F), Fisherman's Wharf's most authentic attraction. Moored along Hyde St Pier, the three most interesting are the 1891 schooner *Alma*, which hosts guided sailing trips in summer; 1890 steamboat *Eureka*; and iron-hulled *Balclutha*, which brought coal to San Francisco. It's free to walk the pier; pay only to board ships.

Fisherman's Wharf Food Trucks

Two side-by-side food trucks near the corner of Jones and Jefferson Sts are perfect alternatives to the Wharf's over-priced restaurants: **Codmother** (📞 415-606-9349; www.codmother. com; 496 Beach St; mains $7-13; ⏰ 11am-5pm Mon & Wed-Fri, to 11:30am-6pm Sat & Sun; 🚌 47, 🚃 Powell-Mason, Ⓜ F) serves fish and chips, plus Baja-style fish tacos; while **Tanguito** (📞 415-577-4223; 2850 Jones St; dishes $4-13; ⏰ 11:30am-6:30pm Tue-Fri, noon-7:30pm Sat, to 6pm Sun; 🚌 47, 🚃 Powell-Mason, Ⓜ F) makes its own Argentinian-style empanadas with chicken or steak. Note early closing times and outdoor-only seating.

USS Pampanito

The **USS Pampanito** (📞 415-775-1943; www.maritime.org; Pier 45; adult/child/family $20/10/45; ⏰ 9am-8pm, can vary seasonally; 👶; 🚌 19, 30, 47, 🚃 Powell-Hyde, Ⓜ E, F), a WWII-era US Navy submarine, completed six wartime patrols that sank six Japanese ships and damaged four others, and lived to tell the tale. Submariners' stories of tense moments in underwater stealth mode will have you holding your breath, and all those cool brass knobs and mysterious hydraulic valves will make 21st-century technology seem overrated.

SS Jeremiah O'Brien

It's hard to believe that the historic 10,000-ton **SS Jeremiah O'Brien** (📞415-554-0100; www.ssjeremiah obrien.org; Pier 45; adult/child/family $20/10/45; ⏰10am-4pm; 🚻; 🚌19, 30, 47, 🚋Powell-Hyde, Ⓜ E, F) was turned out by San Francisco's shipbuilders in under eight weeks. Harder still to imagine how she dodged U-boats on a mission delivering supplies to Allied forces on D-Day. Of the 2710 Liberty ships launched during WWII, it is one of only two still fully operational. Check the website for upcoming four-hour cruises.

Aquatic Park

Fisherman's Wharf's eccentricity is mostly staged, but at **Aquatic Park** (📞415-561-7000; www.nps.gov/safr; admission free; 🚻; 🚌19, 30, 47, 🚋Powell-Hyde) it's the real deal: extreme swimmers dive into the bone-chilling waters of the bay in winter, while oblivious old men cast fishing lines and listen to AM-radio sports. Aside from being the city's principal swimming beach (with bathrooms, but no lifeguard), the park is ideal for people-watching and sandcastle building. For perspective on the Wharf, wander out along the enormous Municipal Pier at the foot of Van Ness Ave.

Aquatic Park Bathhouse (Maritime Museum)

The **Maritime Museum** (Aquatic Park Bathhouse; www.maritime.org; 900 Beach St; admission free; ⏰10am-4pm; 🚻; 🚌19, 30, 47, Powell-Hyde) was

Ghirardelli Square

built as a casino and public bathhouse in 1939 by the Depression-era Works Progress Administration (WPA). Beautifully restored murals depict the mythical lands of Atlantis and Mu and the handful of exhibits include maritime ephemera and dioramas. Note the entryway slate carvings by celebrated African American artist Sargent Johnson and the back veranda's sculptures by Beniamino Bufano.

Ghirardelli Square

Willy Wonka would tip his hat to Domingo Ghirardelli, whose business became the West's largest chocolate factory in 1893. After the company moved to the East Bay, developers reinvented the factory as a mall and ice-cream parlor in 1964. Today, **Ghirardelli Square** (☏ 415-775-5500; www.ghirardellisq.com; 900 North Point St; ☺ 10am-9pm; 🚌 19, 30, 47, 🚋 Powell-Hyde) has entered its third incarnation as a boutique time-share/spa complex with wine-tasting rooms. The square looks quite spiffy, with local boutiques and, of course, **Ghirardelli Ice Cream** (☏ 415-474-3938; www. ghirardelli.com; 900 North Point St, Ghirardelli Sq; ice creams $11-16; ☺ 8:30am-11pm Sun-Thu, to midnight Fri & Sat; 👪; 🚌 19, 30, 47, 🚋 Powell-Hyde).

Fishermen at Pier 47

A few third- and fourth-generation fishermen remain in the bay, but to withstand the drop in salmon and other local stocks some now use their boats for tours, surviving off the city's new lifeblood: tourism. Find the remaining fleet around Pier 47.

Explore ⊕

Downtown, Civic Center & SoMa

Downtown has all the urban amenities: art galleries, swanky hotels, malls and entertainment megaplexes. Civic Center is a zoning conundrum, with great performances and Asian art treasures on one side of City Hall and dive bars and soup kitchens on the other. In artsy, techie South of Market (SoMa), everyone gets down on the dance floor.

The Short List

○ **Ferry Building (p54)** *Grazing the NorCal food scene with bay views.*

○ **San Francisco Museum of Modern Art (p56)** *Getting lost in mesmerizing installation art.*

○ **San Francisco Symphony (p68)** *Watching impresario Michael Tilson Thomas conduct from the tips of his toes.*

○ **Asian Art Museum (p61)** *Venturing across the Pacific via the museum's treasures.*

○ **Embarcadero** *People-watching and checking out the dazzling views of the Bay Bridge.*

Getting There & Around

Streetcar Historic F-Market streetcars run along Market St, as does BART.

🚌 Buses 2, 5, 6, 7, 14, 19, 21, 27, 30, 31, 38, 41, 45 and 47 serve downtown and/or SoMa.

Ⓜ Metro lines run under Market St. N goes to Caltrain station. T runs from downtown, via SoMa, stopping along 3rd St.

Neighborhood Map on p58

View of San Francisco Museum of Modern Art (p56) from Yerba Buena

Top Experience 📷

Trawl the Market Stalls at the Ferry Building

San Francisco puts its love of food front and center at the Ferry Building. The once-grand port was overshadowed by a 1950s elevated freeway – until the overpass collapsed in 1989's Loma Prieta earthquake. The Ferry Building survived and became a symbol of San Francisco's reinvention, marking your arrival onto America's forward-thinking food frontier.

◉ MAP P58, H3

www.ferrybuildingmarketplace.com

cnr Market St & the Embarcadero

🕑 10am-7pm Mon-Fri, 8am-6pm Sat, 11am-5pm Sun

🚌 2, 6, 9, 14, 21, 31,
Ⓜ Embarcadero,
Ⓑ Embarcadero

Then & Now

The Ferry Building's trademark 240ft tower welcomed dozens of ferries daily after its 1898 inauguration. But with the opening of the Bay and Golden Gate Bridges, ferry traffic subsided in the 1930s. An overhead freeway was built, obscuring the building's stately facade and turning it black with exhaust fumes. Only after the 1989 earthquake did city planners realize this was the perfect place for a new public commons.

Today the grand arrivals hall tempts commuters to miss the boat and get on board with SF's latest culinary trends instead. Indoor kiosks sell locally roasted espresso, artisan cheese and cured meats, plus organic ice-cream flavors to match. Award-winning restaurants and bars further entice visitors to stick around and raise a toast to San Francisco.

Farmers Market

Before the Ferry Building's renovations were completed in 2003, the **Ferry Plaza Farmers Market** (📞415-291-3276; www.cuesa.org; street food $3-12; ⏰10am-2pm Tue & Thu, from 8am Sat; ☂️♿) began operating out front on the sidewalk. Soon the foodie action spread to the bayfront plaza, drawing 50 to 100 local food purveyors. While locals grumble over high prices, there's no denying that the Ferry Plaza market offers seasonal and sustainable treats and produce.

Bay Bridge Lights

The Bay Bridge looms large on the horizon south of the Ferry Building. In 2013 lighting artist Leo Villareal strung 25,000 LED lights onto the vertical suspension cable of the bridge's western span, transforming it into a 1.8-mile light show. Each night, the lights blink in never-repeating patterns – one second the bridge looks like bubbly champagne, then a lava-lamp forest, then Vegas-style fountains. And although the installation was meant to be temporary, hypnotized local donors made it permanent in 2016.

★ Top Tips

○ The Saturday morning farmers market offers the best people-watching – it's not uncommon to spot celebrities.

○ Arrive early if you're shopping, before those pesky *Top Chef* contestants snap up the best finds.

✗ Take a Break

The Ferry Building is foodie central, with options ranging from food trucks and Ferry Plaza farmers market finds on the south side to oysters and bubbly at **Hog Island Oyster Company** (📞415-391-7117; www.hogislandoysters.com; 6 oysters $19-21; ⏰11am-9pm).

Top Experience 📷

Explore the San Francisco Museum of Modern Art

The expanded San Francisco Museum of Modern Art (SFMOMA) is a mind-boggling feat, nearly tripling in size to accommodate a sprawling collection of modern and contemporary artworks over seven floors – but SFMOMA has defied limits since its founding in 1935. It was an early investor in then-emerging art forms like photography, installations, video, digital art and industrial design.

👁 MAP P58, E3

www.sfmoma.org

151 3rd St

adult/child $25/free

🕐 10am-5pm Fri-Tue, to 9pm Thu, atrium from 8am Mon-Fri

🚌 5, 6, 7, 14, 19, 21, 31, 38, Ⓜ Montgomery, Ⓑ Montgomer

New Galleries, Expanding Collections

Even during the Depression, SFMOMA envisioned a world of vivid possibilities, starting in San Francisco. The collection has outgrown its home twice since then, and the 2016 expansion offers access to its art-filled ground-floor galleries. The unprecedented long-term loan of more than 1100 postwar and contemporary works by the Fisher Family (founders of SF-based clothiers the Gap, Old Navy and Banana Republic) was one catalyst behind Snøhetta architects' $305 million expansion, which added shipshape galleries around the original Mario Botta–designed building and iconic oculus.

Suggested Itinerary

There are free gallery tours, but exploring on your own inspires the thrill of discovery, which is what SFMOMA is all about. Following this itinerary, you should be able to cover collection highlights in two to four hours. Start on the 3rd floor with SFMOMA's standout **photography** collection and special exhibitions. Meditate amid serene paintings in the **Agnes Martin room** surrounded by 4th-floor abstract art, then get an eyeful of Warhol's **Pop Art** on the 5th floor.

Head to the 6th floor for an exhibition of **German art** after 1960, and then hit the 7th floor for a showcase of cutting-edge contemporary works and intriguing media arts installations. Head downstairs via the atrium to see how SFMOMA began, with colorful local characters admiring equally colorful works by Diego Rivera, Frida Kahlo and Henri Matisse on the 2nd floor.

★ **Top Tips**

◦ For weekend visits and special exhibits, book tickets ahead online.

◦ Visitors under age 18 enjoy free admission, but they must have a ticket for entry.

✗ **Take a Break**

Sunny days are ideal for restorative coffee and impromptu panini in the rooftop cafe and sculpture garden.

0
0
400 m
0.2 miles

1

McAllister St

🌟 19 Larkin St

Hyde St

Ellis St

Leavenworth St

✖ 9

Van Ness Ave

Elm St

Polk St

Geary St

🌟 18

Grove St

Golden Gate Ave

Tenderloin Museum Walking Tours

Turk St

⊙ 11

O'Farrell St

⊙ 12

Mason St

20 🌟

Dr Carlton B Goodlett Pl

2

Hayes St

Larkin St

Asian Art Museum

Civic Center Plaza

⊙ 5

McAllister St

Jones St

Eddy St

Glide Memorial United Methodist Church

Fell St

United Nations Plaza

Luggage Store Gallery

Taylor St

⊙ 13

Powell St Cable Car Turnaround

Ⓜ Market St Ⓜ

Civic Center

Stevenson St

⊙ 3

Club OMG

Ⓜ Powell St

Jessie St

Jessie St

3

Mission St

Minna St

⊙ 23

10th St

Grace St

9th St

8th St

7th St

Natoma St

Howard St

Mary St

6th St

5th St

Tehama St

Tehama St

Clementina St

4

11th St

Dore Al

Langton St

16 ⊙

Moss St

Russ St

Harriet St

Folsom St

SOUTH OF MARKET (SOMA)

Oasis

Powerhouse

Dandyhorse SF Bike Tours

Shipley St

Clara St

Eagle Tavern

Harrison St

Stud

Victoria Manalo Draves Park

14 ⊙

Harrison St

10th St

9th St

8th St

James Lick Skwy

Morris St

Bryant St

5

7th St

Gilbert St

Harriet St

6th St

5th St

Brannan St

Bluxome St

Townsend St

6

For reviews see

⊙	Top Experiences	p54
⊙	Sights	p60
✖	Eating	p62
⊙	Drinking	p65
🌟	Entertainment	p68
🔒	Shopping	p70

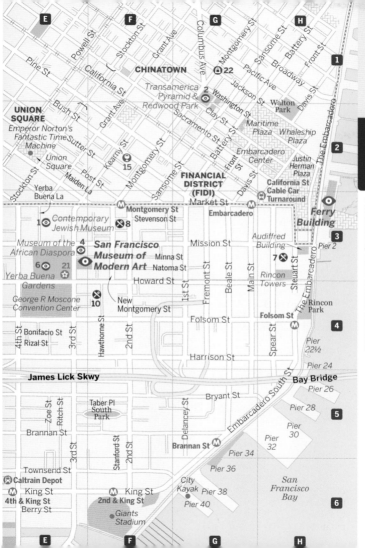

E **F** **G** **H**

Powell St
Pine St
Stockton St
Grant Ave
CHINATOWN
Columbus Ave
Montgomery St
Sansome St
Battery St
Front St
California St
Broadway
Pacific Ave
🔒 22
Jackson St
Walton Park
Bush St
Transamerica Pyramid & Redwood Park
2 Washington St
Davis St
Clay St
Maritime Plaza
Whaleship Plaza

UNION SQUARE
Emperor Norton's Fantastic Time Machine
Sutter St
Grant Ave
Kearny St
Sacramento St
Battery St
Front St
Embarcadero Center
Justin Herman Plaza

Union Square
Post St
🚇 15
Montgomery St
Sansome St
Davis St
California St Cable Car Turnaround

Stockton St
Maiden La
Yerba Buena La

FINANCIAL DISTRICT (FIDI)
Market St
Embarcadero
Ferry Building

Montgomery St
Stevenson St
1 ◉ Contemporary Jewish Museum
✕ 8
Mission St
Audiffred Building
Pier 2

Museum of the African Diaspora
4 ◉
San Francisco Museum of Modern Art
Minna St
Natoma St
Howard St
7 ✕ Steuart St
Rincon Towers

6 ◉ 21 ✪
Yerba Buena Gardens
1st St
Fremont St
Beale St
Main St
Rincon Park

George R Moscone Convention Center
✕ 10
New Montgomery St
Folsom St
Folsom St

Bonifacio St
Rizal St
4th St
3rd St
Hawthorne St
2nd St
Harrison St
Spear St
Pier 22½
Pier 24

James Lick Skwy
Bay Bridge
Pier 26

Zoe St
Ritch St
Taber Pl
South Park
Bryant St
Delancey St
Embarcadero South St
Pier 28
Pier 30

Brannan St
3rd St
Stanford St
2nd St
Brannan St
Pier 32
Pier 34

Townsend St
🚇 Caltrain Depot
City Kayak
Pier 36
San Francisco Bay

🚇 King St
4th & King St
Berry St
🚇 King St
2nd & King St
Giants Stadium
Pier 38
Pier 40

E **F** **G** **H**

1 **2** **3** **4** **5** **6**

Sights

Contemporary
Jewish Museum MUSEUM

1 ◎ MAP P58, E3

The upended blue-steel box miraculously balancing on one corner atop the Contemporary Jewish Museum is appropriate for an institution that upends conventional ideas about art and religion. Architect Daniel Libeskind designed this museum to be rational, mystical and powerful: building onto a 1907 brick power station, he added blue-steel elements to form the Hebrew word *l'chaim* (life). But it's the contemporary art commissions that truly bring the building to life. (☎415-655-7856; www.thecjm.org; 736 Mission St; adult/student/child $14/12/free, after 5pm Thu $8; ⏰11am-5pm Mon, Tue & Fri-Sun, to 8pm Thu; ♿; ☷14, 30, 45, Ⓜ Montgomery, Ⓑ Montgomery)

Transamerica
Pyramid &
Redwood Park NOTABLE BUILDING

2 ◎ MAP P58, G1

The defining feature of San Francisco's skyline is this 1972 pyramid, built atop a whaling ship abandoned in the gold rush. A half-acre redwood grove grows out front, on the site of Mark Twain's favorite saloon and the newspaper office where Sun Yat-sen drafted his Proclamation of the Republic of China. Although these transplanted redwoods have shallow roots, their intertwined structure helps them reach dizzying heights – Twain himself couldn't have penned a more perfect metaphor for San Francisco. (www.thepyramidcenter.com; 600 Montgomery St; ⏰10am-3pm Mon-Fri; Ⓜ Embarcadero, Ⓑ Embarcadero)

Luggage
Store Gallery GALLERY

3 ◎ MAP P58, C3

Like a dandelion pushing through sidewalk cracks, this plucky nonprofit gallery has brought signs of life to one of the Tenderloin's toughest blocks for two decades. By giving SF street artists a gallery platform, the Luggage Store helped launch graffiti-art star Barry McGee, muralist Rigo and street photographer Cheryl Dunn. Find the graffitied door and climb to the 2nd-floor gallery, which rises above the street without losing sight of it.

Among the Luggage Store regulars you might recognize around town are Brazilian duo Osgemeos, who painted the daredevil graffiti artist leaping off the side of the Luggage Store building, and Clare Rojas, who created the Warfield Theater mural of women exchanging gifts across generations. With such poignant streetwise works and regular community arts events, this place puts the tender in the Tenderloin. (☎415-255-5971; www.luggagestoregallery.org; 1007 Market St; ⏰noon-5pm Wed-Sat; ☷6, 7, 9, 21, Ⓜ Civic Center, Ⓑ Civic Center)

Museum of the African Diaspora

MUSEUM

4 ◉ MAP P58, E3

MoAD assembles an international cast of characters to tell the epic story of diaspora, including a moving video of slave narratives told by Maya Angelou. Standouts among quarterly changing exhibits have included homages to '80s New Wave icon Grace Jones, architect David Adjaye's photographs of contemporary African landmarks and Alison Saar's sculptures of figures marked by history. Public events include poetry slams, Yoruba spiritual music celebrations and lectures examining the legacy of the Black Panthers' free school breakfast program. (MoAD; ☎415-358-7200; www.moadsf.org; 685 Mission St; adult/student/child $10/$5/free; ⊙11am-6pm Wed-Sat, noon-5pm Sun; P 🚻; 🚌14, 30, 45, Ⓜ Montgomery, Ⓑ Montgomery)

Asian Art Museum

MUSEUM

5 ◉ MAP P58, B2

Imaginations race from subtle Chinese ink paintings to seductive Hindu temple carvings and from elegant Islamic calligraphy to cutting-edge Japanese minimalism across three floors spanning 6000 years of Asian art. Besides the largest collection of Asian art outside Asia – 18,000 works – the museum offers excellent programs for all ages, from shadow-puppet shows and tea tastings with star chefs to mixers with cross-cultural DJ mash-ups.

Contemporary Jewish Museum

Best Guided Tours

Dandyhorse SF Bike Tours (Map p58, B4; ☏ 415-890-2453; www.dandysftours.com; 33 Gordon St; tours from $69; ☉8am-7pm; ☒12, 19, 27, 47) The ultimate embodiment of San Francisco's DIY spirit, local resident Nick Normuth custom-built a bunch of bikes, studied up on the city and started this cycling tour.

Tenderloin Museum Walking Tours (Map p58, C2; ☏ 415-351-1912; www.tenderloinmuseum.org; 398 Eddy St; adult/with museum admission/night tour $10/15/20; ☉2pm Tue-Sun, 21+ night tour 6pm 1st & 3rd Wed; Ⓜ Powell, Ⓑ Powell, ☒ Powell-Mason, Powell-Hyde) Resident Tenderloin Museum historians lead intrepid visitors past groundbreaking Tenderloin locales.

Emperor Norton's Fantastic Time Machine (Map p58, E2; ☏ 415-548-1710; www.sftimemachine.com; $30; ☉11am Thu & Sat, waterfront tour 11am Sun; ☒ 30, 38, Ⓜ Powell St, Ⓑ Powell St, ☒ Powell-Mason, Powell-Hyde) Follow the self-appointed Emperor Norton (aka historian Joseph Amster) across 2 miles of dastardly, scheming, uplifting and urban-legendary SF terrain.

(☏415-581-3500; www.asianart.org; 200 Larkin St; adult/student/child $15/10/free, 1st Sun of month free; ☉10am-5pm Tue, Wed & Fri-Sun, to 9pm Thu; ♿; Ⓜ Civic Center, Ⓑ Civic Center)

Yerba Buena Gardens   PARK

6 ◉ MAP P58, E3

Breathe a sigh of relief: you've found the lush green hideaway in the concrete heart of SoMa, between Yerba Buena Center for the Arts and Metreon entertainment complex. This is a prime spot to picnic, hear free noontime summer concerts (see website) or duck behind the fountain for a smooch. The Martin Luther King Jr Memorial Fountain is a wall of water that runs over the Reverend's immortal words: '…until justice rolls down like water and righteousness like a mighty stream.' (☏415-820-3550; www.yerbabuena gardens.com; cnr 3rd & Mission Sts; ☉6am-10pm; ♿; Ⓜ Montgomery, Ⓑ Montgomery)

Eating

Yank Sing   DIM SUM $

7 ✗ MAP P58, H3

San Francisco's most iconic dim sum experience has earned its accolades, and remains the go-to choice for its pork and broth-filled Shanghai dumplings and unparalleled Peking duck by the slice. The cart service is efficient and impeccable, and the kind staff members speak English, Cantonese and Mandarin. Reservations are a must. (📞415-781-1111; www.yanksing.com; 101 Spear St; dim sum plates $6-14; ⏱11am-3pm Mon-Fri, 10am-4pm Sat & Sun; 🚌6, 9, 14, 21, 31, Ⓜ Embarcadero, Ⓑ Embarcadero)

Sentinel

SANDWICHES $

8 🍴 MAP P58, F3

Rebel SF chef Dennis Leary revolutionizes the humble sandwich with top-notch seasonal ingredients: lamb gyros get radical with pesto and eggplant, and corned beef crosses borders with Swiss cheese and house-made Russian dressing. Check the website for daily menus and call in your order,

or expect a 10-minute wait – sandwiches are made to order. Enjoy in nearby Yerba Buena Gardens. (📞415-769-8109; www.thesentinel sf.com; 37 New Montgomery St; sandwiches $9-12; ⏱7am-2:30pm Mon-Fri; 🚌12, 14, Ⓜ Montgomery, Ⓑ Montgomery)

Liholiho Yacht Club

HAWAIIAN, CALIFORNIAN $$

9 🍴 MAP P58, D1

Who needs yachts to be happy? Aloha abounds over Liholiho's pucker-up-tart cocktails and gleefully creative Calwaiian/Hawafornian dishes – surefire mood enhancers include spicy beef-tongue *bao* (Chinese steamed buns), duck-liver mousse with pickled pineapple on brioche,

Dim sum, Yank Sing

ANTHONY PIDGEON / LONELY PLANET ©

San Francisco's Homeless

It's inevitable: panhandlers will ask you for spare change during your visit to San Francisco, especially around Union Sq and downtown tourist attractions. This is nothing new.

Some historians date San Francisco's challenges with homelessness to the 1940s, when shell-shocked WWII Pacific Theater veterans were discharged here without sufficient support. Wherever the problem started, today homeless populations forced out of other cities come to San Francisco for its milder climate, history of tolerance and safety-net services.

Since 2004, the city has doubled what it spends on the homelessness problem (to a cool $300 million a year). On the streets, though, the problem feels worse than ever: the opioid epidemic has spilled addicts onto the streets, while gentrification has triggered homeless migrations within the city. Because of San Francisco's growing income inequality, the problem may get worse before it gets any better.

To help out, you can volunteer with or make a donation to a San Franciscan homeless-services organization like **Glide** (Map p58, D2; 415-674-6090; www.glide.org; 330 Ellis St; celebrations 9am & 11am Sun; 38, MPowell, BPowell), or you could offer your services to an organization back home. Homelessness isn't a uniquely San Franciscan problem – it's a global human tragedy.

and Vietnamese slaw with tender squid and crispy tripe. Reservations are tough; arrive early or late for bar dining, or head downstairs to Louie's Gen-Gen Room speakeasy for shamelessly tasty bone-marrow-butter waffles. (415-440-5446; www.lycsf.com; 871 Sutter St; dishes $11-37; 5-10:30pm Mon-Thu, to 11pm Fri & Sat; 2, 3, 27, 38, California)

Benu   CALIFORNIAN, FUSION $$$

10 MAP P58, F4

SF has pioneered Asian fusion cuisine for 150 years, but the pan-Pacific innovation chef-owner Corey Lee brings to the plate is gasp-inducing: foie-gras soup dumplings – what?! Dungeness crab and truffle custard pack such outsize flavor into Lee's faux–shark's fin soup, you'll swear Jaws is in there. A Benu dinner is an investment, but don't miss star sommelier Yoon Ha's ingenious pairings ($210). (415-685-4860; www.benusf.com; 22 Hawthorne St; tasting menu $310; 5:30-8:30pm Tue-Thu, to 9pm Fri & Sat; 10, 12, 14, 30, 45)

Drinking

Bourbon & Branch
BAR

11 🚇 MAP P58, D2

'Don't even think of asking for a cosmo' reads the House Rules at this Prohibition-era speakeasy, recognizable by its deliciously misleading Anti-Saloon League sign. For award-winning cocktails in the liquored-up library, whisper the password ('books') at the O'Farrell entrance. Reservations required for front-room booths and Wilson & Wilson Detective Agency, the noir-themed speakeasy-within-a-speakeasy (password supplied with reservations). (📞 415-346-1735; www.bourbonandbranch.com; 501 Jones St; 🕓 6pm-2am; 🚌 27, 38)

Zombie Village
COCKTAIL BAR

12 🚇 MAP P58, D2

San Francisco probably didn't need anymore tiki bars, but we're certainly not going to complain about Zombie Village, the latest from Future Bars Group, also behind Bourbon & Branch, Rickhouse and Local Edition. Guests step off the gritty Tenderloin streets and into a dark and mystical tiki wonderland, where the rum flows like wine and skulls are everywhere.

An upstairs voodoo lounge features a bar of skulls and a pseudo-cave room is illuminated with candles. The space also includes eight semi-private tiki huts (must be reserved in advance) that are perfect for group drinking. Chief Lapu Lapu serves up to five people

Craft beer

LUKASZ WISNIEWSKI / EYEEM / GETTY IMAGES ©

SoMa's Best LGBTIQ+ Bars

Sailors have cruised Polk St and gay/trans joints in the Tenderloin since the 1940s, the Castro's gay bars boomed in the 1970s and the Mission has been a magnet for lesbians since the '60s – but SoMa warehouses have been the biggest weekend LGBTIQ+ scene for decades.

Eagle Tavern (Map p58, A4; www.sf-eagle.com; 398 12th St; cover $5-10; ⏱5pm-2am Mon-Thu, from 2pm Fri, from noon Sat & Sun; 🚌9, 12, 27, 47) Legendary leather bar with Sunday beer busts.

Oasis (Map p58, A4; 📞415-795-3180; www.sfoasis.com; 298 11th St; tickets $15-35; 🚌9, 12, 14, 47, Ⓜ Van Ness) SF's dedicated drag cabaret mounts outrageous shows.

Stud (Map p58, B4; 📞415-863-6623; www.studsf.com; 399 9th St; cover $5-8; ⏱5pm-2am Tue-Thu, 5pm-4am Fri, 7pm-4am Sat, 7pm-2am Sun; 🚌12, 19, 27, 47) Draws a crowd at night with its surreal, only-in-SF theme events.

Powerhouse (Map p58, A4; 📞415-522-8689; www.powerhouse-sf.com; 1347 Folsom St; cover free-$10; ⏱4pm-2am Sun-Thu, from 3pm Fri & Sat; 🚌9, 12, 27, 47) Major men-only back-patio action.

Club OMG (Map p58, C3; 📞415-896-6473; www.clubomgsf.com; 43 6th St; cover free-$10; ⏱5-10pm Tue, to 2am Thu & Fri, 7pm-2am Sat; Ⓜ Powell, Ⓑ Powell) Dance in your skivvies on Skid Row.

with rum, passion fruit, orange and vanilla, and it can be set on fire. (📞415-474-2284; www.thezombie village.com; 441 Jones St; ⏱5pm-2am Mon-Fri, from 6pm Sat; 🚌27, 38)

Aunt Charlie's Lounge
LGBTIQ+, CLUB

13 🗺 MAP P58, C2

Vintage pulp-fiction covers come to life when the Hot Boxxx Girls storm the battered stage at Aunt Charlie's on Friday and Saturday nights at 10:15pm ($5; call for reservations). Thursday is Tubesteak Connection ($5, free before 10pm), when bathhouse anthems and '80s disco draw throngs of less formal types. Other nights bring guaranteed minor mayhem, seedy glamour and Tenderloin dive-bar shenanigans. Cash only. (📞415-441-2922; www.auntcharlies lounge.com; 133 Turk St; cover free-$5; ⏱noon-2am Mon-Fri, 10am-2am Sat, 10am-midnight Sun; 🚌27, 31, Ⓜ Powell, Ⓑ Powell)

EndUp

LGBTIQ+, CLUB

14 🚇 MAP P58, C4

Forget Golden Gate Bridge – once you EndUp watching the sunrise over the 101 freeway ramp from this rollicking dance club's backyard oasis (complete with leafy waterfall), you've officially arrived in SF. Dance sessions are marathons fueled by EndUp's 24-hour license, so Saturday nights have a way of turning into Monday mornings. Laughable bathrooms; serious weapon/drug checks. (☎415-646-0999; www.facebook.com/theendup; 401 6th St; cover $10-60; ⏰11pm Fri-8am Sat, 10pm Sat-4am Mon; 🚍12, 19, 27, 47)

Pagan Idol

LOUNGE

15 🚇 MAP P58, F2

Flirt with disaster over a Hemingway is Dead: rum, bitters and grapefruit served in a skull. Despite the novelty glassware, tiki isn't a new trend in SF – shipping-route cocktails date from the 1800s, and Pagan Idol's are thoroughly researched. So place your order while volcanoes erupt in the back corner, and brace for impact – these tiki cocktails are no joke. (☎415-985-6375; www.paganidol.com; 375 Bush St; ⏰4pm-2am Mon-Fri, from 6pm Sat; Ⓜ F, J, K, L, M, Ⓑ Montgomery)

Downtown, Civic Center & SoMa Drinking

Aunt Charlie's Lounge

ROBERT CLAY / ALAMY ©

Sightglass Coffee CAFE

16 📞 MAP P58, C4

Follow cult coffee aromas into this sunny SoMa warehouse, where family-grown, high-end coffee is roasted daily. Aficionados sip signature Owl's Howl Espresso downstairs or head to the mezzanine Affogato Bar to get ice cream with that espresso. Daredevils should try the sparkling coffee cascara shrub – soda made with the cherry fruit of coffee plants. Sister operations have opened in the Haight, the Mission, SFMOMA and the Ferry Plaza Farmer's Market. (📞415-861-1313; www.sightglasscoffee.com; 270 7th St; ⏱7am-7pm; 🚌12, 14, 19, Ⓜ Civic Center, Ⓑ Civic Center)

Entertainment

San Francisco Symphony CLASSICAL MUSIC

17 ⭐ MAP P58, A2

From the moment conductor Michael Tilson Thomas bounces up on his toes and raises his baton, the audience is on the edge of their seats for another thunderous performance by the Grammy-winning SF Symphony. Don't miss signature concerts of Beethoven and Mahler, live symphony performances with such films as *Star Trek*, and creative collaborations with artists from Elvis Costello to Metallica. (📞box office 415-864-6000, rush-ticket hotline 415-503-5577; www.sfsymphony.org; Grove St, btwn Franklin St & Van Ness Ave; tickets

War Memorial Opera House

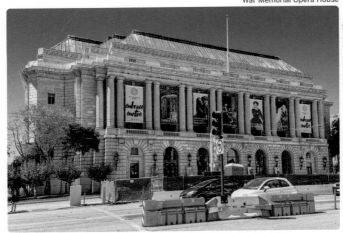

V_E / SHUTTERSTOCK ©

$20-150; 🚌21, 45, 47, Ⓜ Van Ness, Ⓑ Civic Center)

San Francisco Opera OPERA

18 ⭐ MAP P58, A2

Opera was SF's gold-rush soundtrack – and SF Opera rivals the Met, with world premieres of original works ranging from Stephen King's *Dolores Claiborne* to *Girls of the Golden West,* filmmaker Peter Sellars' collaboration with composer John Adams. Expect haute-couture costumes and radical sets by painter David Hockney. Score $10 same-day standing-room tickets at 10am; check website for Opera Lab pop-ups. (📞415-864-3330; www.sfopera.com; 301 Van Ness Ave, War Memorial Opera House; tickets from $10; 🚌21, 45, 47, 49, Ⓜ Van Ness, Ⓑ Civic Center)

Great American Music Hall LIVE MUSIC

19 ⭐ MAP P58, C1

Everyone busts out their best sets at this opulent 1907 bordello turned all-ages venue – indie rockers like the Band Perry throw down, international legends such as Salif Keita grace the stage, and John Waters hosts Christmas extravaganzas. Pay $25 extra for dinner with prime balcony seating to watch shows comfortably, or rock out with the standing-room scrum downstairs. (📞415-885-0750; www.gamh.com; 859 O'Farrell St; shows $20-45; 🕐box office

The Great American Music Hall

STEVE JENNINGS/GETTY IMAGES ©

noon-6pm Mon-Fri, 5pm-close on show nights; ♿; 🚌19, 38, 47, 49)

San Francisco Ballet DANCE

The USA's oldest ballet company is looking sharp in more than 100 shows annually, from *The Nutcracker* (the US premiere was here) to modern originals. Performances are at the War Memorial Opera House (see **18** ⭐ Map p58, A2) from January to May, and you can score $15 to $20 same-day standing-room tickets at the box office (open four hours before curtain on performance days only). (📞tickets 415-865-2000; www.sfballet.org; 301 Van Ness Ave, War Memorial Opera House; tickets $22-150; 🕐ticket sales over the phone 10am-4pm Mon-Fri; 🚌5, 21, 47, 49, Ⓜ Van Ness, Ⓑ Civic Center)

American Conservatory Theater THEATER

20 ⭐ MAP P58, D2

Breakthrough shows launch at this turn-of-the-century landmark, which has hosted ACT's productions of Tony Kushner's *Angels in America* and Robert Wilson's *Black Rider*, with William S Burroughs' libretto and music by Tom Waits. Major playwrights like Tom Stoppard, Dustin Lance Black and Eve Ensler premiere work here, while the ACT's newer Strand Theater, on Market St, stages more experimental works. (ACT; ☑ 415-749-2228; www.act-sf.org; 405 Geary St; ☺ box office 10am-6pm Mon, to curtain Tue-Sun; ☒ 8, 30, 38, 45, ☒ Powell-Mason, Powell-Hyde, Ⓜ Powell, Ⓑ Powell)

Yerba Buena Center for the Arts PERFORMING ARTS

21 ⭐ MAP P58, E3

Rock stars would be jealous of art stars at YBCA openings, which draw overflowing crowds of art-school groupies with shows ranging from cyberpunk video art to hip-hop showdowns and Indian kathak–American tap-dance fusion freestyle. Most touring dance and jazz companies perform at YBCA's main theater (across the sidewalk from the gallery). (YBCA; ☑ 415-978-2700; www.ybca.org; 700 Howard St; tickets free-$25; ☺ box office 11am-6pm Tue, Wed, Fri-Sun, to 8pm Thu, galleries closed Mon; ♿; ☒ 14, Ⓜ Powell, Ⓑ Powell)

Shopping

William Stout Architectural Books BOOKS

22 🅰 MAP P58, G1

You can't fit SFMOMA into your pocket, but you can put it on your coffee table – California architectural obsessions begin at William Stout, with 1st-edition catalogs for SFMOMA designers Snøhetta

---

Attending a Giants Game

The downside of the **Giants'** (AT&T Park; Map p58, F6; ☑ 415-972-2000, tours 415-972-2400; http://sanfrancisco.giants.mlb.com; 24 Willie Mays Plaza; tickets $14-349, stadium tour adult/child/senior $22/12/17; ☺ tour times vary; ♿; Ⓜ N, T) winning streak is that games often sell out, even though the stadium is among America's most expensive ballparks. Don't despair: season-ticket holders sell unwanted tickets through the team's Double Play Ticket Window (see website).

If you can't find tickets, consider renting a **kayak** (p40) to paddle around McCovey Cove and wait for a 'splash hit.' Or head to the park's eastern side along the waterfront, where you may be able to stand at the archways and watch innings for free.

MICHAEL LEE / GETTY IMAGES ©

AT&T Park, home of the San Francisco Giants

and retro classics like *Cabins, Love Shacks and Other Hide-outs*. This is SF's best-kept design secret, where Apple designers and skateboard makers alike find inspiration at reasonable prices. (☎415-391-6757; www.stoutbooks. com; 804 Montgomery St; ☼10am-6:30pm Mon-Fri, to 5:30pm Sat; 🚌1, 10, 12, 41, 🚋California)

Barbary Coast Dispensary CANNABIS

23 🔒 MAP P58, D3

At a time when most San Francisco dispensaries still feel like clinics and give off a buzz-killing, prescription-only vibe, Barbary Coast Dispensary feels decidedly recreational. The red tufted booths and antique chandeliers will have you feeling like you stepped into a steampunk Victorian apothecary, and the staff, known as budtenders, are friendly people who know their weed. (☎415-243-4400; www. barbarycoastsf.com; 952 Mission St; ☼8am-9:45pm; 🚌6, 7, 9, 14, Ⓜ Powell, Ⓑ Powell)

Explore ◈
North Beach & Chinatown

Dumplings and rare teas are served under pagoda roofs on Chinatown's main streets – but its historic back alleys are filled with temple incense, mah-jongg tile clatter and distant echoes of revolution. Wild parrots circle over the Italian cafes and bohemian bars of North Beach, where enough espresso is served to fuel your own Beat poetry revival.

The Short List

○ **Chinatown alleyways (p80)** *Hearing mah-jongg tiles and temple gongs as you wander story-filled backstreets.*

○ **Coit Tower (p74)** *Climbing Filbert Street Steps past heckling parrots and fragrant gardens to this panoramic, mural-lined tower.*

○ **City Lights Books (p80)** *Reflecting in the Poet's Chair and celebrating free speech.*

○ **Chinese Historical Society of America (p80)** *Time-traveling at this museum, housed in the historic Julia Morgan–designed Chinatown YWCA.*

○ **Li Po (p86)** *Picking up where Jack Kerouac and Allen Ginsberg left off at a historic Beat hangout.*

Getting There & Around

Muni The T line streetcar service links Chinatown and North Beach to downtown and Dogpatch.

🚌 Key routes through Chinatown and North Beach are 1, 10, 12, 30, 39, 41 and 45.

🚋 Powell-Mason and Powell-Hyde lines serve these hoods. The California St cable car passes through the southern end of Chinatown.

Neighborhood Map on p78

Top Experience 📷
Survey the City from Coit Tower

The exclamation point on San Francisco's skyline is Coit Tower, built as a monument to firefighters by eccentric heiress Lillie Hitchcock Coit. This concrete projectile became a lightning rod for controversy during the Great Depression – but no matter your perspective, the tower's viewing platform panoramas are breathtaking.

◎ MAP P78, E2

📞 415-249-0995

www.sfrecpark.org

Telegraph Hill Blvd

nonresident elevator fee adult/child $8/5, mural tour full/2nd fl only $8/5

🕙 10am-6pm Apr-Oct, to 5pm Nov-Mar

🚌 39

WPA Murals

The tower's lobby murals depict city life during the Depression: people lining up at soup kitchens, organizing dockworkers' unions, partying despite Prohibition and reading books – including Marxist manifestos – in Chinese, Italian and English.

When they were completed in 1934, these federally funded artworks were controversial. Authorities denounced the 26 artists that painted them as communists, but San Franciscans embraced the murals as symbols of the city's openness. In 2012 voters passed a measure to preserve them as historic landmarks, and today the murals are freshly restored – and as bold as ever.

Viewing Platform

For a parrot's-eye panoramic view of San Francisco 210ft above the city, take the elevator to the tower's open-air platform. Book your docent-led, 30- to 40- minute mural tour online – tour all murals ($8), or just the seven hidden stairwell murals ($5).

Filbert Street Steps

In the 19th century, a ruthless entrepreneur began quarrying and blasting away roads on the side of Telegraph Hill. City Hall eventually stopped the quarrying, but the view of the bay from the Filbert Street Steps is still (wait for it) dynamite.

Napier Lane

Along the steep climb from Sansome St up Filbert Street Steps toward Coit Tower, stop for a breather along Napier Lane, a wooden boardwalk lined with cottages and gardens where wild parrots have flocked for decades.

★ **Top Tips**

○ To glimpse seven restored murals up a hidden stairwell on the 2nd floor, reserve a docent-led tour online.

○ Don't miss the 360-degree viewing-platform panorama.

✕ **Take a Break**

Stop by Liguria Bakery (p84) for focaccia hot from a 100-year-old oven on your way up Telegraph Hill – and enjoy a picnic that'll make the parrots jealous.

North Beach & Chinatown Survey the City from Coit Tower

Walking Tour 🥾

North Beach Beat

Discover the old stomping ground of the motley crowd of writers, artists, dreamers and unclassifiable characters Jack Kerouac once called 'the mad ones.'

Walk Facts
Start City Lights Books
End Li Po
Length 1.5 miles; two hours

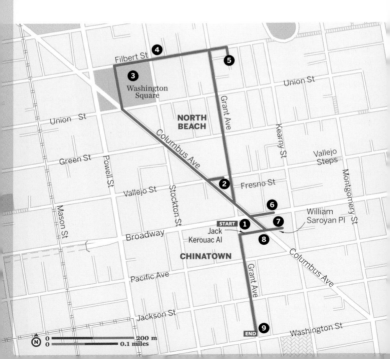

❶ City Lights Books

At **City Lights Books** (p80), home of Beat poetry and free speech, pick up something to inspire your journey into literary North Beach – Ferlinghetti's *San Francisco Poems* and Ginsberg's *Howl* make excellent company.

❷ Caffe Trieste

Head to **Caffe Trieste** (p88) for opera on the jukebox and potent espresso in the back booth, where Francis Ford Coppola drafted *The Godfather* screenplay.

❸ Washington Square

At **Washington Square** (p83), you'll spot parrots in the treetops and octogenarians in tai chi tiger stances on the lawn – pure poetry in motion.

❹ Liguria Bakery

At the corner, **Liguria Bakery** (p84) will give you something to write home about: focaccia hot from a century-old oven.

❺ Bob Kaufman Alley

Peaceful **Bob Kaufman Alley** (👣; 🚌8, 10, 12, 30, 41, 45, 🚋Powell-Mason, Ⓜ️T) was named for the street poet who kept a 12-year vow of silence that lasted until the Vietnam War ended – when he finally walked into a North Beach cafe and recited his poem 'All Those Ships That Never Sailed.'

❻ Beat Museum

Dylan jam sessions erupt in the bookshop, Allen Ginsberg spouts poetry nude in backroom documentary screenings, and stoned visitors grin beatifically at it all. Welcome to the **Beat Museum** (p80), spiritual home to all 'angelheaded hipsters burning for the ancient heavenly connection' (to quote Ginsberg's *Howl*).

❼ Specs

The obligatory literary bar crawl begins at **Specs** (p87) amid merchant-marine memorabilia, tall tales from old-timers, and pitchers of Anchor Steam.

❽ Vesuvio

Jack Kerouac once blew off Henry Miller to go on a bender at **Vesuvio** (p87), until bartenders ejected him into the street now named for him: Jack Kerouac Alley (p82). Note the words of Chinese poet Li Po embedded in the alley: 'In the company of friends, there is never enough wine.'

❾ Li Po

Follow the lead of Kerouac and end your night under the laughing Buddha at **Li Po** (p86) – there may not be enough wine, but there's plenty of beer.

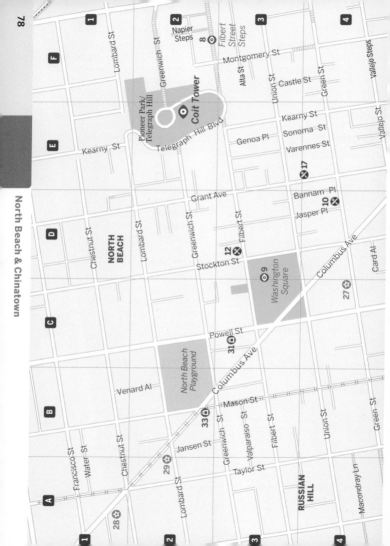

North Beach & Chinatown

1

F

Lombard St

Greenwich St

Napier Steps

8

Filbert Street Steps

2

Montgomery St

3

Alta St

Union St

Castle St

Green St

Vallejo Steps

4

Pioneer Park/ Telegraph Hill

Coit Tower

E

Kearny St

Telegraph Hill Blvd

Genoa Pl

Kearny St

Sonoma St

Varennes St

Vallejo St

17 ✕

Grant Ave

Bannam Pl

Jasper Pl

10 ✕

Chestnut St

D

Lombard St

NORTH BEACH

Greenwich St

Filbert St

12 ✕

Stockton St

Washington Square

9 ✪

Columbus Ave

Card Al

27 ✪

C

Powell St

31 ▣

Columbus Ave

North Beach Playground

Venard Al

B

Mason St

33 ▣

Greenwich St

Jansen St

Valparaiso St

Filbert St

Union St

Green St

Francisco St

Water St

Chestnut St

A

Lombard St

29 ✪

Taylor St

RUSSIAN HILL

Macondray Ln

28 ✪

1

2

3

North Beach & Chinatown

Montgomery St

5

Beat
Museum-Broadway 4
Romolo Pl 25
City Lights 2
Books
Jack 7
Kerouac Alley
23 26
13

Pacific Ave
24
Columbus Ave 16
18
21 20
22
Beckett St
Grant Ave
Jackson St 30
Stockton St
Stone St
11

6

Chinese
Culture
Center 5

Kearny St
Drag Me
Along Tours
Portsmouth
Square

Mark
Twain St

7

Spring St

8

Kearny St

F

Wentworth Pl
19 15

Red Blossom
Tea Company

CHINATOWN
Commercial St
32
Waverly Pl 14

Sacramento St

Grant Ave

E

Chinatown
Alleyways 1
Tin How 6
Temple

Washington St

Clay St

Chinese Historical
3 Society of America

Chinese
Playground

Joice St

D

Powell St

Broadway

John St

Wetmore St

Sacramento St

C

Ina
Coolbrith
Park Vallejo St

Mason St

Sproule La

NOB
HILL

Auburn St

B

Broadway Tunnel

Taylor St

Jackson St

Bernard St

Pacific Ave

Jones St

Jones St

A

0 N

0 200 m
0 0.1 miles

For reviews see

◈ Top Experiences p74
⊙ Sights p80
✕ Eating p83
✕ Drinking p86
✪ Entertainment p89
▣ Shopping p91

5

6

7

8

Sights

Chinatown Alleyways

AREA

1 ◎ MAP P78, E7

The 41 historic alleyways packed into Chinatown's 22 blocks have seen it all since 1849: gold rushes and revolution, incense and opium, fiery and icy receptions. In these narrow backstreets lined with clinker-brick buildings, temple balconies jut out over bakeries, laundries and barbers – there was nowhere to go but up in Chinatown after 1870, when laws limited Chinese immigration, employment and housing. Chinatown Alleyway Tours (p82) and Chinatown Heritage Walking Tours (p82) offer community-supporting, time-traveling strolls through defining moments in American history. (btwn Grant Ave, Stockton St, California St & Broadway; 🚌1, 30, 45, 🚋Powell-Hyde, Powell-Mason, California)

City Lights Books

CULTURAL CENTER

2 ◎ MAP P78, E5

Free speech and free spirits have rejoiced here since 1957, when City Lights founder and poet Lawrence Ferlinghetti and manager Shigeyoshi Murao won a landmark ruling defending their right to publish Allen Ginsberg's epic poem *Howl*. Celebrate your freedom to read freely in the designated Poet's Chair upstairs overlooking Jack Kerouac Alley, load up on zines on the mezzanine and entertain radical ideas downstairs in the Pedagogies of Resistance section. (📞415-362-8193; www.citylights.com; 261 Columbus Ave; ⏰10am-midnight; 🚻; 🚌8, 10, 12, 30, 41, 45, 🚋Powell-Mason, Powell-Hyde, Ⓜ️T)

Chinese Historical Society of America

MUSEUM

3 ◎ MAP P78, D8

Picture what it was like to be Chinese in America during the gold rush, transcontinental railroad construction and Beat heyday in this 1932 landmark, built as Chinatown's YWCA. CHSA historians unearth fascinating artifacts: 1920s silk *qipao* dresses, WWII Chinatown nightclub posters and Frank Wong's Chinatown miniatures. Exhibits share personal insights and historical perspectives on Chinese American historical milestones – including the Civil Rights movement, Cold War and Chinese Exclusion Act, which officially excluded Chinese immigrants from US citizenship and civil rights from 1882 to 1943. (CHSA; 📞415-391-1188; www.chsa.org; 965 Clay St; admission free; ⏰noon-5pm Tue-Fri, 11am-4pm Sat & Sun; 🚻; 🚌1, 8, 30, 45, 🚋California, Powell-Mason, Powell-Hyde, Ⓜ️T)

Beat Museum

MUSEUM

4 ◎ MAP P78, E5

The closest you can get to the complete Beat experience without breaking a law. The 1000-plus artifacts in this museum's literary-ephemera collection include the sublime (the banned edition of

Ginsberg's *Howl,* with the author's own annotations) and the ridiculous (those Kerouac bobblehead dolls are definite head-shakers). Downstairs, watch Beat-era films in ramshackle theater seats redolent with the odors of literary giants, pets and pot. Upstairs, pay your respects at shrines to individual Beat writers. A seismic retrofit may mean closures; call ahead. (📞800-537-6822; www.kerouac.com; 540 Broadway; adult/student $8/5, walking tours $30; ⏱museum 10am-7pm, walking tours 2-4pm Sat; 🚌8, 10, 12, 30, 41, 45, 🚋Powell-Mason, Ⓜ T)

Chinese Culture Center

GALLERY

5 ◎ MAP P78, F7

You can see all the way to China from the Hilton's 3rd floor inside this cultural center, which hosts exhibits ranging from showcases of contemporary Chinese ink-brush painters to installations of kung-fu punching bags studded with fighting words.

In odd-numbered years, don't miss Present Tense Biennial, where 30-plus Bay Area artists present personal takes on Chinese culture. Visit the center's satellite gallery at 41 Ross Alley for contemporary collaborations; for local historical perspectives, book the center's Chinatown Heritage Walking Tours. (📞415-986-1822; www.cccsf.us; 750 Kearny St, Hilton Hotel, 3rd fl; suggested donation $5; ⏱during exhibitions 10am-4pm Tue-Sat; ♿; 🚌1, 8, 10, 12, 30, 41, 45, 🚋California, Powell-Mason, Powell-Hyde, Ⓜ T)

City Lights Books

Touring Chinatown

On two-hour **Chinatown Alleyway Tours** (☎415-984-1478; www.chinatownalleywaytours.org; Portsmouth Sq; adult/student $26/16; ⏰tours 11am Sat; ♿; 🚌1, 8, 10, 12, 30, 41, 45, 🚋California, Powell-Mason, Powell-Hyde), teenage Chinatown residents guide you through backstreets that have seen it all: Sun Yat-sen plotting China's revolution, '49ers squandering fortunes on opium, services held in temple ruins after the 1906 earthquake. Your presence here helps the community remember its history and shape its future – Chinatown Alleyway Tours are a nonprofit, youth-led program of the Chinatown Community Development Center. Credit cards are accepted for advance online reservations only; drop-ins should bring exact change, because guides don't carry cash.

Local-led, kid-friendly **Chinatown Heritage Walking Tours** (☎415-986-1822; https://tour.cccsf.us; 750 Kearny St, Chinese Culture Center, Hilton Hotel, 3rd fl; adult $30-40, student $20-30; ♿; 🚌1, 8, 10, 12, 30, 41, 45, 🚋California, Powell-Mason, Powell-Hyde) wind through backstreets to key historic sights, including the Golden Gate Fortune Cookie Factory, Tin How Temple and Portsmouth Sq. Tours follow one of two themes: Chinatown History and Food Walk, covering Chinatown's daily life and cultural influence, or Dynasty to Democracy, exploring Chinatown's efforts for rights, justice and opportunity for all. Proceeds support the nonprofit **Chinese Culture Center** (p81); make bookings online or by phone three days in advance.

Tin How Temple

TEMPLE

 6 👁 MAP P78, E7

Atop the barber shops, laundries and diners lining Waverly Place, you'll spot lantern-festooned balconies of temples – including Tin How Temple, built in 1852. Its altar miraculously survived the 1906 earthquake. To pay your respects, follow sandalwood-incense aromas up three flights of stairs. Entry is free, but offerings are customary for temple upkeep. No photography inside, please. (Tien Hau Temple; 125 Waverly Pl; donation customary;

⏰10am-4pm, except holidays; 🚌1, 8, 30, 45, 🚋California, Powell-Mason, Powell-Hyde)

Jack Kerouac Alley

STREET

 7 👁 MAP P78, E5

'The air was soft, the stars so fine, the promise of every cobbled alley so great...' This ode by the *On the Road* and *Dharma Bums* author is embedded in his namesake alley, a fittingly poetic, streetwise shortcut between Chinatown and North Beach via his favorite haunts City Lights (p80), Vesuvio (p87) and a stool near the golden Buddha statue at Li Po (p86) – Kerouac was a true believer in literature, Buddhism and beer. (btwn Grant & Columbus Aves; 🚌8, 10, 12, 30, 41, 45, 🚋Powell-Mason)

Filbert Street Steps

ARCHITECTURE

8 ◉ MAP P78, F2

Halfway through the steep climb up the Filbert Street Steps to Coit Tower, you might wonder if it's all worth the trouble. Take a breather and notice the scenery you're passing: sweeping Bay Bridge vistas, hidden cottages along Napier Lane's wooden boardwalk, and sculpture-dotted gardens in bloom year-round. If you need further encouragement, the wild parrots in the trees have been known to interject a few choice words your gym trainer would probably get sued for using. (🚌39)

Washington Square

PARK

9 ◉ MAP P78, D3

Wild parrots, tai chi masters and nonagenarian churchgoing *nonnas* (grandmothers) are the local company you'll keep on this lively patch of lawn. This was the city's earliest official park, built in 1850 on the ranchland of pioneering entrepreneur and San Francisco founder Juana Briones – there's a bench dedicated to her. Parrots keep their distance in the treetops, but like anyone else in North Beach, they can probably be bribed into friendship with a focaccia from Liguria

Bakery (p84), on the square's northeastern corner. (www.sfrecpark. org/washington-square; cnr Columbus Ave & Union St; 🚌8, 30, 39, 41, 45, 🚋Powell-Mason, Ⓜ T)

Eating

Golden Boy

PIZZA $

10 ✖ MAP P78, D4

'If you don't see it don't ask 4 it' reads the menu – Golden Boy has kept punks in line since 1978, serving Genovese focaccia-crust pizza that's chewy, crunchy and hot from the oven. You'll have whatever second-generation Sodini family *pizzaioli* (pizza-makers) are making and like it – especially pesto and clam-and-garlic. Grab square slices and draft beer at the

Golden Boy

JAMES KIRKIKIS / SHUTTERSTOCK ©

bomb-shelter counter and boom: you're golden. (☏415-982-9738; www.goldenboypizza.com; 542 Green St; slices $3.25-4.25; ⏱11:30am-midnight Sun-Thu, to 2am Fri & Sat; ☐8, 30, 39, 41, 45, ☐Powell-Mason)

Good Mong Kok DIM SUM $

11 ✖ MAP P78, D7

Ask Chinatown neighbors about their go-to dim sum and the answer is either grandma's or Good Mong Kok. Lines snake out the door of this counter bakery for dumplings whisked from vast steamers into takeout containers to enjoy in Portsmouth Sq. The menu changes by the minute/hour, but expect classic pork *siu mai*, shrimp *har gow* and BBQ pork buns; BYO chili sauce and black vinegar. (☏415-397-2688; 1039 Stockton St; dumpling orders $2-5; ⏱7am-6pm; ☐30, 45, ☐Powell-Mason, California, Ⓜ T)

Liguria Bakery BAKERY $

12 ✖ MAP P78, D3

Bleary-eyed art students and Italian grandmothers line up by 8am for cinnamon-raisin focaccia hot out of the 100-year-old oven, leaving 9am dawdlers a choice of tomato or classic rosemary and garlic. Latecomers, beware: when they run out, they close. Take yours in waxed paper or boxed for picnics – just don't kid yourself that you're going to save some for later. Cash only. (☏415-421-3786; 1700 Stockton St; focaccia $4-6; ⏱8am-2pm Tue-Fri, 7am-2pm Sat, 7am-noon Sun; ✐♿; ☐8, 30, 39, 41, 45, ☐Powell-Mason, Ⓜ T)

Molinari DELI $

13 ✖ MAP P78, D5

Observe this quasi-religious North Beach noontime ritual: enter Molinari, and grab a number and a crusty roll. When your number's called, let wisecracking staff pile your roll with heavenly fixings: milky buffalo mozzarella, tangy sun-dried tomatoes, translucent sheets of prosciutto di Parma, slabs of legendary house-cured salami, drizzles of olive oil and balsamic. Enjoy hot from the panini press at sidewalk tables. (☏415-421-2337; www.molinarisalame.com; 373 Columbus Ave; sandwiches $11-14.50; ⏱9am-6pm Mon-Fri, to 5:30pm Sat; ☐8, 10, 12, 30, 39, 41, 45, ☐Powell-Mason, Ⓜ T)

Mister Jiu's CHINESE, CALIFORNIAN $$

14 ✖ MAP P78, E8

Success has been celebrated in this historic Chinatown banquet hall since the 1880s – but today, scoring a table at Mister Jiu's is reason enough for celebration. Build memorable banquets from chef Brandon Jew's ingenious Chinese/Californian signatures: quail and Mission-fig sticky rice, hot and sour Dungeness crab soup, Wagyu sirloin and tuna heart fried rice. Don't skip dessert – pastry chef Melissa Chou's salted plum sesame balls are flavor bombs. (☏415-857-9688; www.misterjius.com; 28 Waverly Pl; mains $14-45; ⏱5:30-10:30pm Tue-Sat; ☐30, ☐California, Ⓜ T)

Z & Y

SICHUAN $$

15 MAP P78, E6

Graduate from ho-hum sweet-and-sour and middling *mu shu* to sensational Sichuan dishes that go down in a blaze of glory. Warm up with spicy pork dumplings and heat-blistered string beans, take on the housemade *tantan* noodles with peanut-chili sauce, and leave lips buzzing with fish poached in flaming chili oil and buried under red Sichuan chili peppers. Go early; worth the inevitable wait. (📞415-981-8988; www.zandyrestaurant.com; 655 Jackson St; mains $9-20; ⏰11am-9:30pm Sun-Thu, to 10:30pm Fri & Sat; 🚌8, 10, 12, 30, 45, 🚋Powell-Mason, Powell-Hyde, Ⓜ T)

Trestle

CALIFORNIAN $$

16 MAP P78, F6

If you've got a start-up budget but venture capitalist tastes, you're in luck here: $38 brings three courses of tasty, rustic comfort food. You get two options per course – typically soup or salad, meat or seafood, fruity or choco-latey dessert – so you and your date can taste the entire menu. Get the bonus handmade-pasta course ($10). Seating is tight, but the mood's friendly. (📞415-772-0922; www.trestlesf.com; 531 Jackson St; 3-course meals $38; ⏰5:30-10pm Mon-Thu, to 10:30pm Fri & Sat, to 9:30pm Sun; 🚌8, 10, 12, 30, 45, Ⓜ T)

North Beach & Chinatown Eating

Molinari deli

SHAY BAKSTAD / SHUTTERSTOCK ©

Tea Tasting

Several Grant Ave tea importers let you sample for free, but the hard sell may begin before you finish sipping. For a more relaxed, enlightening teatime experience, **Red Blossom Tea Company** (Map p78, E7; ☏ 415-395-0868; www. redblossomtea.com; 831 Grant Ave; ◷ 10am-5pm Mon-Thu, to 6pm Fri & Sat, 11am-5pm Sun; ◻ 1, 10, 12, 30, 35, 41, ☒ Powell-Mason, Powell-Hyde, California, ⓜ T) offers half-hour premium tea flights with tips on preparing tea for maximum flavor ($35 for up to four participants). Book ahead at weekends; seating is limited.

Cafe Jacqueline
FRENCH $$$

17 ✖ MAP P78, E4

The terror of top chefs is the classic French soufflé – but since 1979, Chef Jacqueline has been turning out perfectly puffy creations that float across the tongue like fog over the Golden Gate Bridge. With the right person to share that seafood soufflé, dinner could hardly get more romantic... until you order the chocolate version for dessert. (☏ 415-981-5565; 1454 Grant Ave; soufflés per person $15-30; ◷ 5:30-11pm Wed-Sun; ✐; ◻ 8, 30, 39, 41, 45, ☒ Powell-Mason, ⓜ T)

Drinking

Comstock Saloon
BAR

18 ◉ MAP P78, F6

During this 1907 saloon's heyday, patrons relieved themselves in the marble trough below the bar – now you'll have to tear yourself away from Comstock's authentic pisco punch and martini-precursor Martinez (gin, vermouth, bitters, maraschino liqueur). Arrive to toast Emperor Norton's statue at happy hour (4pm to 6pm) and stay for the family meal (whatever kitchen staff is eating). Reserve booths to hear when ragtime-jazz bands play. (☏ 415-617-0071; www. comstocksaloon.com; 155 Columbus Ave; ◷ 4pm-midnight Mon, to 2am Tue-Thu, noon-2am Fri, 11:30am-2am Sat, 11:30am-4pm Sun; ◻ 8, 10, 12, 30, 45, ☒ Powell-Mason, ⓜ T)

Li Po
BAR

19 ◉ MAP P78, E7

Beat a hasty retreat to red-vinyl booths where Allen Ginsberg and Jack Kerouac debated the meaning of life under a golden Buddha. Enter the 1937 faux-grotto doorway and dodge red lanterns to place your order: Tsingtao beer or a sweet, sneaky-strong Chinese mai tai made with baijiu (rice liquor). Brusque bartenders, basement bathrooms, cash only – a world-class dive bar. (☏ 415-982-0072; www.lipolounge.com; 916 Grant Ave; ◷ 2pm-2am; ◻ 8, 30, 45, ☒ Powell-Mason, Powell-Hyde, ⓜ T)

Specs

BAR

20 MAP P78, E5

The walls here are plastered with merchant-marine memorabilia, and you'll be plastered too if you try to keep up with the salty characters holding court in back. Surrounded by seafaring mementos – including a massive walrus organ over the bar – your order seems obvious: pitcher of Anchor Steam, coming right up. Cash only. (Specs Twelve Adler Museum Cafe; ☎ 415-421-4112; 12 William Saroyan Pl; ⏰ 5pm-2am Mon-Fri; 🚌 8, 10, 12, 30, 41, 45, 🚋 Powell-Mason, Ⓜ T)

Devil's Acre

BAR

21 MAP P78, E5

Potent potions and lip-smacking quack cures are proudly served at this apothecary-style Barbary Coast saloon. Tartly quaffable Lachlan's Antiscorbutic (lime, sea salt, two kinds of gin) is a surefire cure for scurvy and/or sobriety; when in doubt, go Call a 'Treuse (Chartreuse, lemon, vanilla, egg white). There's happy hour until 7pm, but no food; switch to nonalcoholic 'remedies' (soda with herbal tinctures). (☎ 415-766-4363; www.thedevilsacre.com; 256 Columbus Ave; ⏰ 5pm-2am Tue, from 3pm Wed-Sat, 2pm-midnight Sun, 5pm-midnight Mon; 🚌 8, 10, 12, 30, 41, 45, 🚋 Powell-Mason, Ⓜ T)

Vesuvio

BAR

22 MAP P78, E5

Guy walks into a bar, roars and leaves. Without missing a beat, the bartender says to the next

Vesuvio

KRIS DAVIDSON / LONELY PLANET ©

customer, 'Welcome to Vesuvio, honey – what can I get you?' Jack Kerouac blew off Henry Miller to go on a bender here and, after you've joined neighborhood characters on the stained-glass mezzanine for 8pm microbrews or 8am Kerouacs (rum, tequila and OJ), you'll see why. (☏415-362-3370; www.vesuvio. com; 255 Columbus Ave; ⏰8am-2am; 🚌8, 10, 12, 30, 41, 45, 🚋Powell-Mason)

Caffe Trieste CAFE

23 🚇 MAP P78, E5

Poetry on bathroom walls, opera on the jukebox, live accordion jams and Beat poetry on bathroom

walls: Caffe Trieste has been North Beach at its best since the 1950s. Linger over legendary espresso and scribble your screenplay under the Sardinian fishing mural just as young Francis Ford Coppola did. Perhaps you've heard of the movie: *The Godfather*. Cash only. (☏415-392-6739; www.caffetrieste. com; 601 Vallejo St; ⏰6:30am-10pm Sun-Thu, to 11pm Fri & Sat; 📶; 🚌8, 10, 12, 30, 41, 45, Ⓜ️T)

Réveille CAFE

24 🚇 MAP P78, F6

If this sunny flat-iron storefront doesn't lighten your mood, cap-puccino with a foam-art heart

Exploring the Barbary Coast

In the mid-19th century you could start a San Francisco bar crawl with smiles and 10¢ whiskey – and end up two days later involuntarily working on a ship bound for Patagonia. Now that double-crossing barkeep Shanghai Kelly is no longer a danger to drinkers, revelers can relax at North Beach's once-notorious Barbary Coast saloons. These days you can pick your own poison: historically correct cocktails at **Comstock Saloon** (p86), cult California wines in the backroom speakeasy at **Pawn Shop** (www.thepawnshopsf.com) and enough microbrewed beer at **Magnolia Brewery** (p149) to keep you snoring to Patagonia and back.

Feel like you might need a chaperone? How about bona-fide legend and gold-rush burlesque star Countess Lola Montez (reincarnated in drag by SF historian Rick Shelton)? With **Drag Me Along Tours** (Map p78, F7; ☏415-857-0865; www.dragmealongtours.com; Portsmouth Sq; $30; ⏰tours 11am Sun; 🚌1, 8, 10, 12, 30, 41, 45, 🚋California, Powell-Mason, Powell-Hyde, Ⓜ️T), her Highness leads you through Chinatown alleyways where Victorian ladies made and lost reputations, past North Beach saloons where sailors were shanghaied. Barbary Coast characters gambled, loved and lived dangerously – expect adult content. Reservations required; cash only.

will. Réveille's coffee is like San Francisco on a good day: nutty and uplifting, without a trace of bitterness. Check the circular marble counter for just-baked chocolate-chip cookies and sticky buns. No wi-fi makes for easy conversation, and sidewalk-facing counters offer some of SF's best people-watching. (📞415-789-6258; www.reveillecoffee.com; 200 Columbus Ave; 🕐7am-6pm Mon-Fri, 8am-5pm Sat & Sun; 🚹🚼; 🚌8, 10, 12, 30, 41, 45, 🚋Powell-Mason, Ⓜ️T)

15 Romolo BAR

25 🍸 MAP P78, E5

Strap on your spurs: it's gonna be a wild Western night at this back-alley Basque saloon squeezed between burlesque joints. The strong slay the Jabberwocky (gin, sherry, bitters, fortified wine), but the brazen Baker Beach (mezcal, manzanilla sherry, apricot, vermouth, lemon) makes grown men blush. Bask in $9 Basque Pincon punch at 5pm to 7:30pm happy hours, and pace yourself with tasty *pintxos* (tapas). (📞415-398-1359; www.15romolo.com; 15 Romolo Pl; 🕐5pm-2am; 🚌8, 10, 12, 30, 41, 45, 🚋Powell-Mason, Ⓜ️T)

Saloon BAR

26 🍸 MAP P78, E5

Blues in a red saloon that's been a dive since 1861 – this is North Beach at its most colorful. Legend has it that when the city caught fire in 1906, loyal patrons saved

Caffe Trieste

the Saloon by dousing it with buckets of hooch. Today it's SF's oldest bar, and blues and rock bands perform nightly plus weekend afternoons. Cash only. (📞415-989-7666; www.sfblues.net; 1232 Grant Ave; live music free-$5; 🕐noon-2am; 🚌8, 10, 12, 30, 41, 45, 🚋Powell-Mason)

Entertainment

Beach Blanket Babylon CABARET

27 ⭐ MAP P78, C4

Snow White searches for Prince Charming in San Francisco: what could possibly go wrong? This Disney-spoof musical-comedy cabaret has been running since 1974, but topical jokes keep it outrageous – and wigs as big as parade floats are gasp-worthy. Spectators must be over 21 to handle racy humor, except at cleverly sanitized Sunday matinees. Reservations essential; arrive one hour early for best seats. (BBB; <img_1 /> 415-421-4222; www. beachblanketbabylon.com; 678 Green St, aka Beach Blanket Babylon Blvd; $30-155; ⊘shows 8pm Wed, Thu & Fri, 6pm & 9pm Sat, 2pm & 5pm Sun; 🚌8, 30, 39, 41, 45, 🚋Powell-Mason, Ⓜ T)

Bimbo's 365 Club LIVE MUSIC

28 ⭐ MAP P78, A1

Get your kicks at this 1931 speakeasy with stiff drinks, bawdy vintage bar murals, parquet dance floors for high-stepping like Rita Hayworth (she was in the chorus line here) and intimate live shows by the likes of Beck, Talib Kweli,

Chris Isaak and Nouvelle Vague. Dress snazzy and bring bucks to tip the powder-room attendant – this is a classy joint. It's 21-plus; two-drink minimum; cash only. (📞415-474-0365; www.bimbos365 club.com; 1025 Columbus Ave; from $20; ⊘box office 10am-4pm; 🚌8, 30, 39, 41, 45, 🚋Powell-Mason, Ⓜ T)

Cobb's Comedy Club COMEDY

29 ⭐ MAP P78, A2

There's no room to be shy at Cobb's, where bumper-to-bumper shared tables make the audience cozy – and vulnerable. The venue is known for launching local talent and giving big-name acts (Ali Wong, John Oliver, Michelle Wolf) a place to try risky new material. Check the website for shows, drag brunches and showcases like

Fortune cookies

Really Funny Comedians (Who Happen to Be Women). It's 21-plus; two-drink minimum. (☎415-928-4320; www.cobbscomedyclub.com; 915 Columbus Ave; $17-46; ☉box office 1-6pm Wed, 4-6pm Thu-Sun; 🚌8, 30, 39, 41, 45, 🚋Powell-Mason, Ⓜ T)

Shopping

Golden Gate Fortune Cookies   FOOD & DRINKS

30 🅐 MAP P78, E6

Find your fortune at this bakery, where cookies are stamped from vintage presses – just as they were in 1909, when fortune cookies were invented for SF's Japanese Tea Garden (p166). Write your own fortunes for custom cookies (50¢ each), or get cookies with regular or risqué fortunes (pro tip: add 'in bed' to regular ones). Cash only; $1 tip for photos. (☎415-781-3956; www.goldengatefortunecookies.com; 56 Ross Alley; ☉9am-6pm; 🚌8, 30, 45, 🚋Powell-Mason, Powell-Hyde, Ⓜ T)

San Francisco Rock Posters & Collectibles   VINTAGE, ART

31 🅐 MAP P78, C3

Are you ready to rock?! Enter this trippy temple to classic rock gods – but leave your lighters at home because these concert posters are valuable. Expect to pay hundreds for first-run psychedelic Fillmore concert posters featuring the Grateful Dead – but you can score bargain handbills for San Francisco acts like Santana, the

Dead Kennedys and Sly and the Family Stone. (☎415-956-6749; www.rockposters.com; 1851 Powell St; ☉10am-6pm Mon-Sat; 🚌8, 30, 39, 41, 45, 🚋Powell-Mason, Ⓜ T)

Kim + Ono   FASHION & ACCESSORIES

32 🅐 MAP P78, E8

Hollywood pinups borrowed their slinky silk-robe style from Chinatown burlesque stars back in the '30s – and now you can rock that retro hottie look in boudoir-to-streetwear designs by Chinatown sister-duo designers Renee and Tiffany. Each Kim + Ono silk charmeuse kimono has something extra: hand-painted blossoms, branches and vines, with the occasional crane peeking over the shoulder. (☎415-989-8588; www.kimandono.com; 729 Grant Ave; ☉10am-6pm Mon-Thu, to 6:30pm Fri & Sun, 10am-8pm Sat; 🚌30, 45, 🚋California, Powell-Mason, Ⓜ T)

Real Old Paper   ART, VINTAGE

33 🅐 MAP P78, B2

See the world from the comfort of your living room with a wall of Real Old Paper finds: vintage travel posters, Dutch *Star Wars* promotions, Pacific WWII rationing propaganda and advertisements for Italian vermouth brands. But wait, there's more: collectors Jennifer and Andrew England are always excited to show you new acquisitions not yet on the walls. (☎415-527-8333; www.realoldpaper.com; 801 Columbus Ave; ☉noon-6pm Tue-Sat; 🚌8, 30, 39, 41, 45, Ⓜ T, 🚋Powell-Mason)

Walking Tour 🥾

Russian & Nob Hill Secrets

Cloud nine can't compare to the upper reaches of Nob Hill and Russian Hill, where hilltop gardens, literary landmarks and divine views await discovery up flower-lined stairway walks. If the climb and the sights don't leave you completely weak in the knees, try staggering back downhill after a couple of Nob Hill cocktails. Now you understand why San Francisco invented cable cars.

Walk Facts

Start Vallejo St Steps

End Tonga Room

Length 1.7 miles; two hours

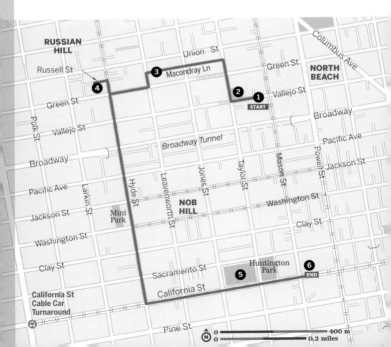

❶ Vallejo Street Steps

Begin your ascent of Russian Hill from North Beach, where **Vallejo Street Steps** (Vallejo St, btwn Mason & Jones Sts; 🚋 Powell-Mason, Powell-Hyde) rise toward Taylor St past Zen gardens and flower-framed apartments. When fog blows, listen for wind chimes and whooshing in the treetops.

❷ Ina Coolbrith Park

Ina Coolbrith was California's first poet laureate, a colleague of Mark Twain and Ansel Adams, and mentor to Jack London and Isadora Duncan. One association she kept secret: her uncle was Mormon prophet Joseph Smith. **Ina Coolbrith Park** (www.sfparks alliance.org/our-parks/parks/ina-coolbrith-park; cnr Vallejo & Taylor Sts; 🚌 41, 45, 🚋 Powell-Mason) is a fitting honor: secret and romantic, with exclamation-inspiring vistas.

❸ Macondray Lane

The route down from Ina Coolbrith Park – via steep stairs, past gravity-defying wooden cottages – looks like a scene from a novel. And so it is: Armistead Maupin used **Macondray Lane** (btwn Jones & Leavenworth Sts; 🚌 41, 45, 🚋 Powell-Mason, Powell-Hyde) as the model for Barbary Lane in *Tales of the City*.

❹ Jack Kerouac's Love Shack

This **modest house** (29 Russell St; 🚌 41, 45, 🚋 Powell-Hyde) witnessed drama in 1951–52, when Jack Kerouac shacked up with Neal and Carolyn Cassady to pound out his 120ft-long scroll draft of *On the Road*. Jack and Carolyn became lovers at Neal's suggestion, but Carolyn frequently kicked them both out.

❺ Grace Cathedral

Hop the Powell-Hyde cable car to Nob Hill's crest, graced by Gothic **Grace Cathedral** (📞 415-749-6300; www.gracecathedral.org; 1100 California St; suggested donation adult/child $3/2; 🕐 8am-6pm Mon-Sat, to 7pm Sun, services 8:30am, 11am & 6pm Sun; 🚌 1, 🚋 California). Labyrinths set a contemplative mood, while stained-glass windows celebrate religious dissidents and scientists.

❻ Tonga Room

There's a 100% chance of tropical rainstorms every 20 minutes inside the **Tonga Room** (📞 reservations 415-772-5278; www.tongaroom.com; 950 Mason St, Fairmont San Francisco; cover $5-7; 🕐 5-11:30pm Sun, Wed & Thu, to 12:30am Fri & Sat; 🚌 1, 🚋 California, Powell-Mason, Powell-Hyde). You'll stay dry in your grass hut, though – the rain only falls on the indoor pool, and cover bands play on an island.

Top Experience 📷

Discover Local History at the Cable Car Museum

That clamor you hear riding cable cars is the sound of San Francisco's peak technology at work. Gears click and wire-hemp ropes whir as these vintage contraptions are hoisted up and over hills too steep for horses or buses – and you can inspect those cables close-up here, in the city's still-functioning cable-car barn.

📞 415-474-1887

www.cablecarmuseum.org

1201 Mason St

donations appreciated

🕐 10am-6pm Apr-Oct, to 5pm Nov-Mar

🚻

🚋 Powell-Mason, Powell-Hyde

Museum Memorabilia

Gearheads, rejoice: three original 1870s cable cars have survived miraculously intact and are still showcased at the Cable Car Museum. The mile-long Clay St cable-car line owned by cable-car inventor Andrew Hallidie is long gone, but the tiny wooden Clay St Railroad Car No 8 dating from 1873 remains the pride and joy of SF.

To demonstrate San Francisco's peak technology, this little car traveled cross-country from Chicago's World Fair to Baltimore railroad yards. Then disaster struck: San Francisco's great 1906 earthquake and fire destroyed most of the city's cable cars and lines. When the Clay St car came home at last for the 1939 Golden Gate Exposition, the city wasn't taking any risks it would be lost again – and kept it safe in deep storage through WWII.

But this cable barn museum isn't just a warehouse for antiques – it's the functioning cable powerhouse that keeps the Powell-Mason line running. Follow the cables running down the street, through an open channel and into the powerhouse, where they wind around massive bull wheels without losing momentum or tension. Head to the upstairs deck to see the powerhouse in action and watch cables whir over the wheels – as awesome a feat of physics now as when Hallidie invented the mechanism in 1873.

Slow Turns

Carnival rides can't compare to the time-traveling thrills of cable cars, San Francisco's steampunk public transit. Novices slide into strangers' laps – cable cars were invented in 1873, long before seat belts – but regulars just grip the leather hand straps, lean back and ride the downhill plunges like pro surfers. Follow their lead, and you'll soon master the San Francisco stance and find yourself conquering the city's hills without even breaking a sweat.

★ **Top Tip**

○ Don't miss the Cable Car Museum shop for SF memorabilia that comes with local street cred. Your purchases of scale-model cable cars and actual cable-car bells help keep this nonprofit museum running and open to all for free.

✗ **Take a Break**

Hop the Powell-Mason or Powell-Hyde line or walk three steep blocks for a peak SF experience: tropical happy hour specials and pupu platters at tiki Tonga Room (p93).

Now that you've seen how cable cars work, it's time to experience one in action. Jump on a south-bound cable car one block over and hang on: the cable car tilts steeply as it climbs the 30-degree grade of Nob Hill and there are no seat belts on the cable car's slippery wooden benches. Grab a hand strap and take the ride standing like a pro surfer and you'll earn honorary San Franciscan status.

When you reach the end of the line at **Powell St Cable Car Turnaround** (www.sfmta.com; cnr Powell & Market Sts; 🚋 Powell-Mason, Mason-Hyde, Ⓜ Powell, Ⓑ Powell), you may breathe a sigh of relief – but for cable-car conductors, this is the toughest moment of the ride. Cable cars can't go in reverse, so they need to be turned around by hand at

the terminus. After you step off the car, turn around to watch cable-car operators as they leap out of the car, grip the chassis of the trolley and slooowly turn the car atop a revolving wooden platform.

Judging the Queue

The best way to secure a spot on a cable car is to board at a turn-around, or cable-car terminus. Lines are shortest to get on the California cable car – the most historic line – but the ride isn't as long or scenic as on the Powell-Mason and Powell-Hyde lines. Powell-Mason cars are quickest to the Wharf, but Powell-Hyde cars traverse more terrain and hills.

Both lines start at the Powell St Turnaround, where riders line up midmorning to early evening,

Powell St Cable Car Turnaround

The Cable Car's Timeless Technology

Legend has it that the idea of cable cars occurred to Andrew Hallidie in 1869, after he watched a horse carriage struggle up Jackson St – and witnessed a terrible crash when one horse slipped on wet cobblestones and the carriage tumbled downhill. Such accidents were considered inevitable on steep San Francisco hills, but Hallidie knew better. His father was the Scottish inventor of wire cable, used to haul ore out of mines during the gold rush. If hemp-and-metal cable was strong enough to haul rocks through High Sierra snowstorms, surely it could transport San Franciscans through fog.

'Wire-rope railway' was a name that didn't inspire confidence, and skeptical city planners granted the inventor just three months to make his contraption operational by August 1, 1873. Hallidie missed his city deadline by four hours when his cable car was poised on Jones St, ready for the descent. Legend has it that the cable-car operator was terrified, so Hallidie himself grabbed the brake and steered the car downhill.

By the 1890s, 53 miles of track crisscrossed the city. Hallidie became a rich man, and he even ran for mayor. But despite his civic contributions and US citizenship, he was defamed as an opportunistic Englishman and lost the race. He remained a lifelong inventor, earning 300 patents and becoming a prominent member of the California Academy of Sciences.

with raucous street performers, doomsday preachers and occasional protesters on the sidelines providing local color. The line at the Friedel Klussman Memorial Turnaround in Fisherman's Wharf is just as long as at Powell St Turnaround, but it thins out rapidly around sunset.

If you're not sure how long the wait will be, count heads and do math: cable cars hold 60 people (29 seated, 31 standing) but depart before they're full to leave room for passengers boarding en route. Cars depart every five to 10 minutes at peak times.

Explore ✣

Japantown, Fillmore & Pacific Heights

Japanese Americans have called this area's quaint Victorians home for over a century, and today Japantown is where cosplay kids come to rock Lolitha Goth fashion at anime premieres. The Fillmore has been a nightlife hub since its 1940s jazz heyday and turned trippy in the psychedelic 1960s. Hilltop Pacific Heights is ringed with mansions owned by people like House Speaker Nancy Pelosi.

The Short List

○ **Fillmore Auditorium (p106)** *Rocking out in SF's shrine to the psychedelic '60s.*

○ **Kabuki Springs & Spa (p103)** *Unwinding in communal Japanese baths.*

○ **Japan Center (p102)** *Slurping ramen, playing anime arcade games and cultivating bonsai gardens.*

○ **Sasa (p103)** *Reaching the next level of Japanese dining with a magic password: omakase.*

○ **Japantown Walking Tour (p102)** *Learning the history of a 'hood that was once a civil rights battleground.*

Getting There & Around

🚃 Lines 1, 2, 3, 10, 22 and 38 serve the area.

🚋 The California line's western terminus is at Van Ness, a few blocks east of Pacific Heights.

Neighborhood Map on p100

Peace Pagoda (p102) WANGCOLIN / SHUTTERSTOCK ©

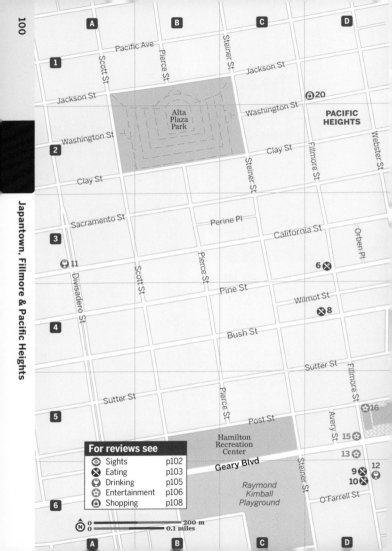

Japantown, Fillmore & Pacific Heights

A **B** **C** **D**

1

Pacific Ave

Scott St

Pierce St

Steiner St

Jackson St

Jackson St

Jackson St

Washington St

🔒20

**PACIFIC
HEIGHTS**

Webster St

2

Washington St

Alta
Plaza
Park

Clay St

Fillmore St

Clay St

Steiner St

Clay St

3

Sacramento St

Perine Pl

California St

Orben Pl

🚇11

Divisadero St

Scott St

Pierce St

Pine St

6✖

Wilmot St

✖8

4

Bush St

Sutter St

Fillmore St

5

Sutter St

Pierce St

Post St

Hamilton
Recreation
Center

Avery St

🎭16

15🎭

13🎭

Geary Blvd

Steiner St

9✖
10✖

12
🛍

For reviews see

⊙	Sights	p102
✖	Eating	p103
🍷	Drinking	p105
🎭	Entertainment	p106
🛍	Shopping	p108

Raymond
Kimball
Playground

O'Farrell St

6

Ⓝ 0 _____ 200 m
0 _____ 0.1 miles

A **B** **C** **D**

E Jackson St **F** **G** **H**

Washington St

1

Lafayette
Park

Clay St

Buchanan St

Gough St

University
of the
Pacific

Clay St

Laguna St

Sacramento St

2

Sacramento St

Franklin St

California St

Pine St

Laguna St

Austin St **3**

Octavia St

14 ☆

Bush St

Gough St

Fern St

Buchanan St

Sutter St

4

Webster St

Japanese Arts &
Cooking Workshops
at JCCNC
◉ 3

Hemlock St

Laguna St

Peter Yorke Way

Sutter St

Post St

JAPANTOWN

🔒 22

🔒 18

19 🔒 ◉ 4 ◉ Japantown Cultural &
Historical Walking Tour

Post St

7 🗡 21 🔒

Japan
Center

◉ 1

🗡 5

Geary Blvd

Starr King Way

5

🔒 17

◉ 2

Peace
Pagoda

Geary Blvd

O'Farrell St

**WESTERN
ADDITION**

Cleary Ct

O'Farrell St

FILLMORE

Gough St

Byington St

Hollis St

Ellis St

Laguna St

Ellis St

6

Ellis St

Willow St

Jefferson
Square

Eddy St

E **F** **G** **H**

Sights

Japan Center NOTABLE BUILDING

1 👁 MAP P100, F5

Time-travel to 1968 as you cross Japan Center's indoor wooden bridges, with *noren* (curtains) and *maneki-neko* (cat figurines) waving welcomes from restaurant entryways. Hard to believe, but this *kawaii*-cute mall started with a knock-down fight. While Japanese American residents were interned during World War II, the city planned to tear down Japantown. Postwar, 1500 recently returned Japantown residents were uprooted to build the mall. But Japantown residents and businesses rallied, stopping evictions and converting the mall into a community hub. (www.sfjapantown.org; 1737 Post St; ⏰10am-midnight; P; 🚍2, 3, 22, 38, 38L)

Peace Pagoda MONUMENT

2 👁 MAP P100, F5

The spiritual center of Japantown's commercial district is minimalist master Yoshiro Taniguchi's Peace Pagoda. It was donated by San Francisco's sister city of Osaka, Japan in 1968. Presented with this five-tiered concrete stupa, San Francisco seemed stupa-fied about what to do with it. Over the years the city clustered shrubs around its stark nakedness, drained leaky reflecting pools and paved over surrounding gardens. Finally, with cherry trees and boulder benches restored to the plaza, the pagoda is in its element, *au naturel.* (Peace Plaza, Japan Center; P; 🚍22, 38)

Japanese Arts & Cooking Workshops at JCCNC COOKING, ARTS

3 👁 MAP P100, E4

Japantown has inspiration to spare – so nonprofit Japanese Cultural and Community Center of Northern California (JCCCNC) generously offers affordable workshops with acclaimed local artisans, chefs and artists. Get hands-on experience with Japanese traditions, such as ikebana, *washi ningyo* (paper dolls), *doburoku* (homebrew sake), *kaiseki* (seasonal meal) cooking and *magawappa* bento box woodcraft. Check the calendar for upcoming events and workshops. (📞415-567-5505; www.jcccnc.org; 1840 Sutter Street; workshops $15-65; ⏰workshop times vary; ♿🚍22,38)

Japantown Cultural & Historical Walking Tour WALKING TOUR

4 👁 MAP P100, F5

Get insider perspectives on Japantown from local National Japanese Historical Society docents sharing cultural insights and personal stories. Tours depart NJAHS Japantown Peace Gallery. From Wednesday to Friday, NJAHS also offers fascinating tours of the Presidio's Fourth Army Intelligence School where Japanese American soldiers were trained

Kabuki Springs & Spa

Gooong! That's a subtle hint to chatty spa-goers to shush, restoring meditative silence to Japantown's communal, clothing-optional **bathhouse** (📞415-922-6000; www.kabukisprings.com; 1750 Geary Blvd; adult $30; ⏱10am-10pm, all-gender Tue, women-identified only Wed, Fri & Sat, men-identified only Mon, Thu & Sat; 🚌22, 38). Salt-scrub in the steam room, soak in the hot pool, take a cold plunge, reheat in the sauna, rinse, and repeat. Men/transmen and women/transwomen alternate days except all-gender Tuesdays, when bathing suits are required. Bath access is $15 with spa treatments, including shiatsu massage.

Plan on two hours minimum for a leisurely bath experience, plus a wait at peak times. Book treatments and bath access online, and arrive promptly – after 15 minutes, you'll be wait-listed. During off-peak weekdays, you can just show up, add your name to the wait list, and browse Japan Center until they text you that there's an opening.

for top-secret missions in WWII and for postwar US occupation of Japan. (📞415-921-5007; www.njahs.org/walking-tours/; NJAHS Japantown Peace Gallery, 1684 Post St; $10-15 per person; ⏱by prior booking Mon-Fri 10am-5pm; ♿; 🚌22, 38)

Eating

Sasa
JAPANESE $

MAP P100, F5

Like an unexpected first-class upgrade, Sasa delights with exceptional attention to detail. Here *katsu* is made with *kurobuta* pork, silken organic *chawanmushi* (egg custard) comes studded with local Dungeness crab, and nigiri sushi showcases thoughtfully sourced delicacies like Santa Barbara sea urchin and Hokkaido scallop.

Trust the *omakase* (chef's tasting menu) – never has a second floor of a mall been this close to heaven. (📞415-683-9674; www.sasasf.com; 22 Peace Plaza, Japan Center, East Wing, 2nd Floor; 6-10 small plates $25-60, individual plates $5-18; ⏱noon-2:30pm & 5:30-9:30 Tue-Sun; 🚌22,38)

Noosh
CALIFORNIAN, TURKISH $

6 ⊗ MAP P100, D3

Follow the spice route into the future with Istanbul-inspired, San Francisco–invented sensations: satiny lamb belly with smoked yoghurt, nutty confit sunchoke kebabs, fermented red pepper and California almond *muhammara* dip. Chef/co-owners Laura and Sayat Ozyilmaz satisfy cravings for something fresh and modern, yet soulful – their signature flatbread with aromatic preserved lemon

Japantown History Walk

In Peace Pagoda Plaza, on the outside wall of Japan Center's east wing, you'll notice an intriguing sign that asks: 'What happened here?' This sign marks the beginning of the Japantown History Walk, a self-guided adventure that takes you around 10 blocks to 17 pivotal locations in Japantown. Take a picture of this sign as a map reference and handy timeline of key events in Japantown's history. Then follow your map to explore the origins of San Francisco sushi, Japanese baseball, WWII internment, civil rights and Japantown's enduring community.

baba ghanoush is so instantly and deeply satisfying, it'll vie for your pizza affections. (📞415-231-5985; 2001 Fillmore St; small plates $5-15; 🪑🚻; 🚌1,22,38)

Marufuku Ramen   RAMEN $

7 ⊗ MAP P100, E5

No Silicon Valley technology excites as much local geekery as a bowl of Marufuku ramen. Its advantages are much discussed: *tonkotsu* broth cooked for 20 hours to achieve milky density, noodles handcut ultra-thin to avoid clumping, topped with egg that's soft-cooked, never hard-boiled. Here's all you need to know: rich, tasty noodles. Value tip: save

some broth and get extra noodles for $2.50. (📞415-872-9786; www.marufukuramen.com/; 1581 Webster St, Suite 235, Japan Center, West Wing, 2nd Floor; $13-17; 🚌22,38)

Out the Door   VIETNAMESE $$

8 ⊗ MAP P100, D4

A casual offshoot of the famous **Slanted Door** (www.slanteddoor.com), home cooking gets an upgrade: brunch brings silken scrambled eggs with five-spice pork belly and cinnamony buttermilk pancakes, while lunch means decadent Dungeness crab cellophane noodles and tangy grapefruit and jicama salad. Reserve online. (OTD; 📞415-923 9575; www.outthedoors.com; 2232 Bush St; mains lunch $14-25, dinner $20-30; ⏱11am-2:30pm & 5:30-9:30pm Mon-Fri, 9am-2:30pm & 5:30-9:30pm Sat & Sun; 🚌2, 3, 22)

State Bird Provisions   CALIFORNIAN $$

9 ⊗ MAP P100, D6

Even before winning multiple James Beard Awards, State Bird attracted lines for 5:30pm seatings not seen since the Dead played neighboring Fillmore Auditorium (p106). Carts arrive tableside laden with California-inspired, dim-sum-sized 'provisions' like jerk octopus and pastrami pancakes. Progress to larger but equally esoteric seasonal signatures, from kimchi-spiced Dungeness crab with bottarga to parmesan-feathered California state bird (quail) atop slow-cooked onions.

Book ahead. (📞415-795-1272; http://statebirdsf.com; 1529 Fillmore St; dishes $8-30; ⏰5:30-10pm Sun-Thu, to 11pm Fri & Sat; 🚌22, 38)

The Progress CALIFORNIAN $$$

10 ❌ MAP P100, D6

The sister bistro of State Bird Provisions seems laid-back – the *wabi-sabi* wooden decor resembles a weatherbeaten boat and Stuart Brioza and Nicole Krasinski's Pacific coastal menu is quintessentially Californian. But surf-meets-turf fare reveals James Beard Award–winning flair – sustainable California sturgeon caviar drifts across potato clouds, while briny Manila clams and earthy roast *maitake* mushrooms bond over squash soup dumplings. Dessert is an afterthought; enjoy

more vegetables. (📞415-673-1294; https://theprogress-sf.com; 1525 Fillmore St; small plates $16-36; ⏰5:30-10pm Sun-Thu, to 11pm Fri & Sat; 🍴; 🚌22, 38)

Drinking

Scopo Divino WINE BAR

11 🍷 MAP P100, A3

Wine, music and conversation blend brunch into happy hour at Scopo Divino. The wine selection does Sonoma proud with old-vine zins and fog-kissed whites, and showcases intriguing Italian blends – take the Taste of Italy flight. Live jazz keeps Fillmore supperclub traditions alive and swinging on Wednesday, Thursday and Sunday. For brunch, pair tart

Japanese cuisine, Japan Center (p102)

SANDRO EID / GETTY IMAGES ©

cherry bellinis with duck confit hash or chicken and waffles. (📞415-928-3728; www.scopodivino. com; 2800 California St; ⏱3-11pm Mon-Fri, 11am-11pm Sat-Sun)

Boba Guys
TEAHOUSE

12 🚇 MAP P100, D6

Ping-pong buddies Andrew and Bin got thirsty and transformed superhero-style into Boba Guys. This is their dream milk tea made with premium small-batch teas and organic milk from Sonoma – plus your choice of tapioca balls or grass jelly made fresh daily. For hangovers, order yours with a side of kimchi fried rice from onsite Sunday Bird pop-up. Expect waits. (www.bobaguys.com; 1522 Fillmore St; ⏱11am-9pm Mon-Thu, noon-11pm Fri & Sat, noon-6pm Sun; 🚌22, 38)

Audium

YHELPMAN / SHUTTERSTOCK ©

Entertainment

Fillmore Auditorium
LIVE MUSIC

13 ⭐ MAP P100, D5

Jimi Hendrix, Janis Joplin, the Grateful Dead – they all played the Fillmore and the upstairs bar is lined with vintage psychedelic posters to prove it. Bands that sell out stadiums keep rocking this historic, 1250-capacity dance hall, and for major shows, free posters are still handed out. To squeeze up to the stage, be polite and lead with the hip. (📞415-346-6000; http:// thefillmore.com; 1805 Geary Blvd; tickets from $20; ⏱box office 10am-3pm Sun, plus 30min before doors open to 10pm show nights; 🚌22, 38)

Audium
SOUNDSCAPE

14 ⭐ MAP P100, H3

Sit in total darkness as Stan Shaff plays his unique musical instrument: an auditorium constructed in 1962 as a living sound sculpture, lined floor to ceiling with 176 speakers. In extended, psychedelic 'room compositions,' meditative tones build to 1970s sci-fi sound effects before resolving into oddly endearing Moog-synthesizer wheezes. A truly San Franciscan experience that induces altered states – prepartying recommended. (📞415-771-1616; www.audium.org; 1616 Bush St; $20; ⏱performances 8:15pm Thur, Fri & Sat; 🚌2, 3, 19, 38, 47, 49, 🚋California)

A Neighborhood Divided

Walk around Japantown, Pacific Heights and the Fillmore and you'll notice these sub-neighborhood distinctions aren't just architectural and cultural – differences of race and class are obvious here. But the history of these three overlapping communities is inextricably linked, and so too is their future.

In the 1880s Japanese American fisherfolk and traders began to settle this quiet hillside. But when Gold Rush billionaires caught a glimpse of the views atop Pacific Heights, they staked out prime sites for grand hilltop mansions. Down below, rapidly constructed Victorian flats were affordable to middle-class Asian, Jewish and African American business owners.

During World War II, President Roosevelt issued Executive Order 9066 requiring that Japanese Americans vacate their homes and report for incarceration in internment camps. Meanwhile, the US needed battleships for war in the Pacific. Women and African Americans took up the shipbuilding effort in Bay Area shipyards, and by 1945, the Fillmore had become a community hub for the city's 30,000 African American workers.

After WWII, Japanese Americans returned from internment to await resettlement – only to discover that the city had other plans for the neighborhood. Redevelopment schemes were extending upmarket Pacific Heights developments downhill, displacing both Japantown and the African American Fillmore district. Over 15 years, more than 38 square blocks of small businesses and historic, affordable family homes were bulldozed. But the community stood its ground. African Americans and Japanese Americans worked together to demand fair housing and civil rights and together stopped the luxury-condo takeover of their neighborhood. Affordable housing was rebuilt and community institutions like the Japanese Cultural and Community Center of Northern California established.

Today as you walk around Japantown and the Fillmore, you'll spot legacy small businesses, nonprofit community centers, historic Victorian flats saved from wrecking balls and mid modern apartment complexes that pioneered affordable housing developments. But the fight to keep this historic city neighborhood economically, culturally and ethnically diverse is ongoing.

Cherry Blossom Festival

Japantown blooms and booms in April, when the Cherry Blossom Festival arrives with *taiko* drums and homegrown hip-hop, yakitori stalls and eye-popping anime cosplay. The biggest West Coast celebration of Japanese culture since 1968, the Cherry Blossom Festival draws 220,000 people over a week of events.

Boom Boom Room
LIVE MUSIC

15 ⭐ MAP P100, D5

Jumping since the '30s, the Boom Boom remains a classic Fillmore venue for blues, soul and funk. Except for the outdoor murals and vintage photos indoors, there's nothing fancy about this joint – curtained stage, Formica tables, bar slinging potent well drinks, well-stomped checkered linoleum dance floor – but it rocks six nights a week with top touring talent. Shows start around 9pm. (☎415-673-8000; www.boomboomroom.com; 1601 Fillmore St; cover varies; ⏱4pm-2am Tue-Sun; 🚌22, 38)

AMC Kabuki 8
CINEMA

16 ⭐ MAP P100, D5

A go-to for rainy day matinees, featuring big-name flicks and film festival favorites. Pro tips: reserve a stadium seat online ($2 extra) and arrive early to beat the line to the bar for wine, beer and well drinks to pair with your movie snacks (hence the 21-plus designation for most shows).

Note: expect a $1.50 to $3 surcharge to see a movie not preceded by commercials. (☎415-346-3243; www.amctheatres.com; 1881 Post St; adult $8 matinee, $16 evening; 🚌2, 3, 22, 38)

Shopping

Kinokuniya Books
BOOKS

17 🔒 MAP P100, E5

Like warriors in a showdown, the *manga*, bookstore and stationery divisions of Kinokuniya vie for your attention. You must choose where your loyalties lie: with vampire comics downstairs, stunning Daido Moriyama photography books and Harajuku street fashion mags upstairs, or across the hall to stationery where whiskey-barrel wood Pure Malt pens and journals featuring a pensive fried egg cartoon character vie for your 'eggsistential thoughts.' (☎415-567-7625; www.kinokuniya.com/us; 1581 Webster St, Japan Center; ⏱10:30am-8pm; 🚌22, 38)

Sanko Kitchen Essentials
CERAMICS, HOMEWARES

18 🔒 MAP P100, F4

Upgrade from ho-hum minimalism with Japanese goods bound to bring joy: bronzed Traveler's Company pen cases, square-handled charcoal Hasami porcelain mugs, Makoo recycled leather totes, old-school Casio calculator watches. Alongside must-have Japanese design objects are original pieces handmade by San Francisco artisans – including those stoneware ramen bowls and bunny chopstick holders. (https://sankosf.com; 1758 Buchanan St; ⊙9am-5pm; 🚌2, 3, 22, 38)

Soko Hardware   HOMEWARES

19 🔒 MAP P100, F5

A Japantown go-to since 1925, Soko has an exceptional selection of hard-to-find housewares, from hot-water ladles for Japanese baths to properly tuned wind chimes. When (not if) Japantown inspires you to bring small graces to your own corner of the world, Soko is your source for essential ikebana, bonsai, tea-ceremony and Zen rock-garden supplies. (📞415-931-5510; 1698 Post St; ⊙9am-5:30pm Mon-Sat; 🚌2, 3, 22, 38)

Margaret O'Leary   CLOTHING

20 🔒 MAP P100, D1

At her flagship store, San Francisco designer Margaret O'Leary showcases whisper-light cardigans of Scottish cashmere and organic cotton ideal for year-round wear in San Francisco. To keep the fog at Bay, layer nubby nautical striped sweaters under hand-knit jackets. For investment pieces, they're fairly priced – and the sale racks hold major scores. (📞415-771-9982;

www.margaretoleary.com; 2400 Fillmore St; ⊙10am-7pm Mon-Sat, 11am-5:30pm Sun; 🚌1, 3, 10, 22, 24)

Katsura Garden   BONSAI

21 🔒 MAP P100, E5

Small wonders are the specialty of Katsura Garden, bonsai garden masters. Years of training go into each tiny tree gracing these shelves, from the miniature juniper that looks like it grew on a windswept molehill to the stunted maple that sheds five tiny, perfect red leaves each autumn. Pick up bonsai and ikebana supplies to keep inspiration flowing. (📞415-931-6209; 1825 Post St, Japan Center; ⊙10am-6pm Mon-Sat, 11am-5:30pm Sun; 🚌2, 3, 22, 38)

Paper Tree   ARTS & CRAFTS

22 🔒 MAP P100, F4

Hang a left at Ruth Asawa's bronze Origami Fountains and discover worlds of possibility. Family-run since 1968, this paper-craft emporium is fueling a local origami revival. Beyond classic paper airplanes and cranes, origami is now used for art (notice the glass-encased paper cocoon-dress), work (Google's self-driving car prototype was origami) and play (fold your own Death Star with the Star Wars kit). (The Origami Store; 📞415-921-7100; 1743 Osaka Way; ⊙10am-5pm Mon & Wed-Sat, 11am-4pm Sun; ♿; 🚌22,38)

Explore ✦
The Mission

The best way to enjoy the Mission is with a book in one hand and a burrito in the other, amid murals, sunshine and the usual crowd of filmmakers, techies, skaters and novelists. Calle 24 (24th St) is SF's designated Latino Cultural District, and the Mission is also a magnet for Southeast Asian Americans, lesbians and dandies.

The Short List

○ **Mission murals (p112)** Seeing garage doors, storefronts and entire alleyways transformed into canvases.

○ **Dolores Park (p118)** Playing, picnicking and people-watching entire days away.

○ **Valencia St (p130)** Strolling the city's liveliest corridor, grabbing a bite at a trendy new restaurant, and popping into novelty stores.

○ **Mission Dolores (p119)** Getting a handle on California history at SF's oldest building, a whitewashed adobe church.

○ **Dogpatch's Creative Corridor (p122)** Appreciating local art, design, wine- and chocolate-making at upstarts.

Getting There & Around

🚌 The Mission, Potrero Hill and the Dogpatch are served by bus lines 14, 22, 49 and 33.

Streetcar The J streetcar heads from downtown through the Mission. The T Muni line from downtown stops along 3rd St, in Potrero's Dogpatch district.

Ⓑ Stations at 16th and 24th Sts serve the Mission.

Neighborhood Map on p116

Mission Dolores (p119) NAEBLYS / SHUTTERSTOCK ©

Top Experience 📷

Check Out the Thought-Provoking Mission Murals

Diego Rivera has no idea what he started. Inspired by the Mexican maestro's 1930s works in San Francisco, generations of Mission muralists have covered alleys and community institutions with 500-plus murals in a splendid show of political dissent, community pride and graffiti-art bravado.

◎ MAP P116, E7

📞 415-285-2287

www.precitaeyes.org

btwn 24th & 25th Sts

🚌 10, 12, 14, 27, 48,

Ⓑ 24th St Mission

Balmy Alley

When 1970s Mission *muralistas* objected to US foreign policy in Latin America, they took to the streets with paintbrushes – beginning with Balmy Alley, pictured left. Bodegas, taquerias and community centers lining 24th St are now covered with murals of mighty Mayan goddesses and Aztec warriors, honoring the district's combined native and Mexican origins.

Clarion Alley

Before Barry McGee and Chris Johansen sold out shows at international art fairs, they could be found at Clarion Alley (p115), gripping spray-paint cans.

Women's Building

In 1993–94 an all-star team of seven women *muralistas* and local volunteers covered the Women's Building (p118) with *Maestrapeace*, featuring icons of female strength.

826 Valencia

Atop literary nonprofit 826 Valencia (p118) is a gold-leafed mural celebrating human attempts to communicate, created by Pulitzer Prize–winning graphic novelist Chris Ware.

Mural Tours

Muralists lead weekend **walking tours** (415-285-2287; www.precitaeyes.org; 2981 24th St; adult $20, child $3; 12, 14, 48, 49, 24th St Mission) covering 60 to 70 Mission murals within a six-to 10-block radius of mural-bedecked Balmy Alley. Tours last one hour to two hours and 15 minutes (for the more in-depth, private Classic Mural Walk). Proceeds fund mural upkeep and overheads at this community arts nonprofit.

★ **Top Tip**

o Public murals are made for discussion and debate – but Mission neighbors take exception to anyone who tags or urinates on them. Murals thoughtlessly defaced can take artists months to restore.

✕ **Take a Break**

Find out why entire Mission art movements have been fueled by burritos at **La Taqueria** (415-285-7117; 2889 Mission St; items $3-11; 11am-8:45pm Mon-Sat, to 7:45pm Sun; 12, 14, 48, 49, 24th St Mission) and *huaraches* (sandal-shaped masa and bean cakes) at La Palma Mexicatessen (p121).

Walking Tour 🚶

Sunny Mission Stroll

On one of the Mission's warm and famously fog-free days, you'll be keeping pace with the locals as you wander the colorful streets of this thriving, traditionally Hispanic (though intensely gentrified) neighborhood. Viewing its elaborate murals, sampling the local delicacies and relaxing in the park, you'll understand why folks of all kinds are now so insistent on living here.

Walk Facts
Start Clarion Alley
End Mission Cheese
Length 1 mile; two hours

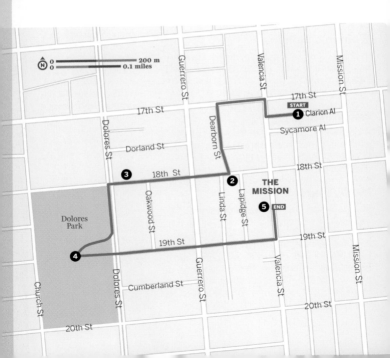

❶ Clarion Alley

Most graffiti artists shun broad daylight – but not in **Clarion Alley** (https://clarionalleymuralproject. org; btwn 17th & 18th Sts; 🚍14, 22, 33, Ⓑ16th St Mission, Ⓜ16th St Mission), SF's street-art showcase. On sunny days, and with prior consent, local street artists paint new murals and touch up tagged works. A few pieces survive for years, such as Megan Wilson's daisy-covered Tax the Rich or Jet Martinez' glimpse of Clarion Alley inside a man standing in a forest.

❷ Women's Building Murals

The nation's first women-owned-and-operated community center has quietly done good work with more than 150 women's organizations since 1979, but the 1994 *Maestrapeace* mural showed the **Women's Building** (p118) for the landmark it truly is. *Muralistas* and volunteers covered the building with goddesses and women trailblazers, including Nobel Prize–winner Rigoberta Menchú, poet Audre Lorde and artist Georgia O'Keeffe.

❸ Bi-Rite Creamery

Velvet ropes at clubs seem pretentious in laid-back San Francisco, but at organic **Bi-Rite Creamery** (📞415-626-5600; www.biritecreamery. com; 3692 18th St; ice creams $3.50-9; 🕙11am-10pm; 🚍33, Ⓑ16th St Mission, Ⓜ) they make perfect sense. The line wraps around the corner for salted-caramel ice cream with house-made hot fudge, or Sonoma honey-lavender ice cream packed into waffle cones. For a quicker fix, get balsamic-strawberry soft serve at the window.

❹ Dolores Park

The Mission's living room is **Dolores Park** (p118), site of semi-professional tanning, free shows and a Mayan-pyramid playground (sorry kids: no blood sacrifice allowed). Join serious soccer games and lazy Frisbee sessions on flat patches. Tennis and basketball courts are open to anyone who's got game. Don't miss downtown panoramas from the hillside benches.

❺ Mission Cheese

Wrought-iron dancing skeletons embedded in Valencia St sidewalks mark your path to **Mission Cheese** (p121). Place your order at the counter, then grab sidewalk seating to gloat over creamy California goat cheeses, sip Sonoma wines and trend-spot Mission street fashion.

The Mission

Brannan St
9th St
SOMArts
F 4

Central Fwy
Market St
Duboce Ave
Clinton Park
Brosnan St
14th St
15th St
Albion St
Guerrero St
Dolores St

Harrison St
Howard St
Folsom St
12th St
13th St
Erie St
11th St
10th St
Treat Ave

Bryant St
Florida St
16th St
17th St
Franklin Square
Catharine Clark Gallery
Hosfelt Gallery
Jack Fischer Gallery

York St
Bryant St
Mariposa St
Florida St
16th
19th St

Alabama St
Harrison St
Treat Ave

Folsom St
15th St
Shotwell St
29
18th St
S Van Ness Ave
Capp St

Harrison St
Folsom St
Shotwell St
S Van Ness Ave
Natoma St
Minna St
Otis St
Adair St
Chile Lindo
16th St Mission
Mission St
37
San Carlos St
Lexington St
Valencia St
14

Hoff St
Rondel Pl
Clarion Al
Sycamore Al
35
Dearborn St
Women's Building
Lapidge St
13
2
19th St

Valencia St
32
25
22
Albion St
26
Creativity Explored
16th St
6
17th St
Dortand St
18 Reasons
Oakwood St
9
39

31
20
21

5
Mission Dolores
18th St
Dolores Park
3

The Mission

THE MISSION

NOE VALLEY

San Francisco General Hospital

826 Valencia

Mission Community Market

Urban Putt

Calle 24 Latino Cultural District

24th St Mission

Mission Cultural Center for Latino Arts

Balmy Alley

Garfield Square

Potrero Ave
Hampshire St
York St
Bryant St
Florida St
Alabama St
Harrison St
Treat Ave
Folsom St
Shotwell St
S Van Ness Ave
Capp St
Mission St
Bartlett St
Valencia St
Guerrero St
Dolores St
Chattanooga St

Potrero Ave
Hampshire St
York St
Bryant St
Harrison St
Treat Ave
Lucky St
Folsom St
Horace St
Virgil St
Cypress St
Capp St
Lilac St
Mission St
Osage St
Cesar Chavez St
Precita Ave

20th St
21st St
22nd St
23rd St
24th St
25th St
26th St

Cumberland St
Liberty St
Fair Oaks St
Quane St
Ames St
Poplar St
San Jose Ave
Orange Al
Elizabeth St
Alvarado St
Hill St

7
30
11
19
17 8
18
28
38 24
36
41 27 33
40
12
10
34
15
23
42
9

For reviews see	
Top Experiences	p112
Sights	p118
Eating	p121
Drinking	p125
Entertainment	p128
Shopping	p131

0   400 m
0   0.2 miles

Sights

826 Valencia

CULTURAL CENTER

1 ◉ MAP P116, B5

Avast, ye scurvy scallywags! If ye be shipwrecked without yer eye patch or McSweeney's literary anthology, lay down ye doubloons and claim yer booty at this here nonprofit pirate store. Below decks, kids be writing tall tales for dark nights a'sea, and ye can study writing movies, science fiction and suchlike, if that be yer dastardly inclination. (☎415-642-5905; www.826valencia.org; 826 Valencia St; ☉noon-6pm; 👶; 🚌14, 33, 49, 🅱16th St Mission, Ⓜ J)

Women's Building

NOTABLE BUILDING

2 ◉ MAP P116, B4

A renowned and beloved Mission landmark since 1979, the nation's first women-owned-and-operated community center is festooned with one of the neighborhood's most awe-inspiring murals. The *Maestrapeace* mural was painted in 1994 and depicts hugely influential women, including Nobel Prize–winner Rigoberta Menchú, poet Audre Lorde, artist Georgia O'Keeffe and former US Surgeon General Dr Joycelyn Elders. (☎415-431-1180; www.womensbuilding.org; 3543 18th St; 🚌14, 22, 33, 49, 🅱16th St Mission, Ⓜ J)

Dolores Park

PARK

3 ◉ MAP P116, A4

Welcome to San Francisco's sunny side, the land of street ball and Mayan-pyramid playgrounds, semiprofessional tanning and taco picnics. Although the grassy expanses are mostly populated by relaxing hipsters, political protests and other favorite local sports do happen from time to time, and there are free movie nights and mime troupe performances in summer. Climb to the upper southwestern corner for superb views of downtown, framed by palm trees. (www.sfrecpark.org/destination/mission-dolores-park; Dolores St, btwn 18th & 20th Sts; ☉6am-10pm; 👶🐾; 🚌14, 33, 49, 🅱16th St Mission, Ⓜ J)

SOMArts

CULTURAL CENTER

4 ◉ MAP P116, F1

All roads in San Francisco's art underground lead to this nonprofit creative community hub under a highway overpass. Shows have featured eviction letters turned into art, Mike Arcega's restatement of Emma Lazarus' Statue of Liberty poem with found objects, and Sean Anomie's long-exposure photos of car taillights. Check the website for info on lively events, openings, literary potlucks and the annual Open Studios show. (☎415-863-1414; www.somarts.org; 934 Brannan St; ☉gallery noon-7pm Tue-Fri, to 5pm Sat; 🚌8, 9, 10, 19, 27, 47)

Mission Dolores

CHURCH

5 ⊙ MAP P116, A3

The city's oldest building and its namesake, whitewashed adobe Misión San Francisco de Asís was founded in 1776 and rebuilt from 1782. Today the modest adobe structure is overshadowed by the ornate adjoining 1913 **basilica**, built after the 1876 brick Gothic cathedral collapsed in the 1906 earthquake. It now features stained-glass windows depicting California's 21 missions and, true to Mission Dolores' name, seven panels depict the Seven Sorrows of Mary. (Misión San Francisco de Asís; ☏415-621-8203; www.missiondolores. org; 3321 16th St; adult/child $7/5; ☉9am-4:30pm May-Oct, to 4pm Nov-Apr; ☐22, 33, ⒷB16th St Mission, ⓂJ)

Creativity Explored

GALLERY

6 ⊙ MAP P116, B3

Brave new worlds are captured in celebrated artworks destined for museum retrospectives, international shows and even Marc Jacobs handbags and CB2 pillowcases – all by local artists with developmental disabilities who create at this nonprofit center. Intriguing themes range from monsters to Morse code, and openings are joyous celebrations with the artists, their families and rock-star fan base. (☏415-863-2108; www.creativityexplored.org; 3245 16th St; donations welcome; ☉10am-5pm Mon-Wed & Fri, to 7pm Thu, noon-5pm Sat; ☐14, 22, 33, 49, ⒷB16th St Mission, ⓂJ)

Dolores Park

JE JIM / GETTY IMAGES ©

Anglim Gilbert Gallery

GALLERY

7 ⦿ MAP P116, F7

The Bay Area hits the big time here, with gallery director Ed Gilbert continuing Anglim's 30-year legacy of launching art movements, from Beat assemblage to Bay Area conceptualists. Major artists range from political provocateur Enrique Chagoya to sublime sculptor Deborah Butterfield, yet shows here maintain a hair-raising edge, such as an upraised fist pushed through gallery walls in David Huffman's *Panther*. (415-433-2710; www.anglimgilbertgallery.com; 1275 Minnesota St, 2nd fl; admission free; 11am-6pm Tue-Sat; 48, T)

Urban Putt

MINIGOLF

8 ⦿ MAP P116, D6

Leave it to the town that brought you Burning Man and the Exploratorium to turn innocent mini-golf games into total trips. Urban Putt's course looks like a Tim Burton hallucination, from tricky windmill Transamerica Pyramid hole 5 to Día de los Muertos–themed hole 9. Enjoy big beers with wee snacks, including mini corndogs and tiny chicken-and-waffle stacks on sticks. (415-341-1080; www.urbanputt.com; 1096 S Van Ness Ave; adult/child $12/8; 4pm-midnight Mon-Thu, to 1am Fri, 11am-1am Sat, to midnight Sun; 14, B 24th St Mission)

18 Reasons

COOKING

9 ⦿ MAP P116, A4

Go gourmet at this Bi-Rite (p115) – affiliated community food nonprofit, offering deliciously educational events: wine tastings, knife-skill and cheese-making workshops, and chef-led classes. Mingle with fellow foodies at family-friendly $12 community suppers and multicourse wine-maker dinners ($95 to $125). The website lists bargain guest-chef pop-ups and low-cost classes with cookbook authors. Spots fill quickly for hands-on cooking classes – book early. (415-568-2710; www.18reasons.org; 3674 18th St; classes & dining events $12-125; ; 22, 33, M J)

Mission Cultural Center for Latino Arts

ART

10 ⦿ MAP P116, C7

Join a class in tango, take up the conga, get crafty with your kids or silkscreen a protest poster at the printmaking studio at the Mission's Latinx arts hub. Teachers are friendly and participants range from *niños* (kids) to *abuelos* (grandparents). Check the online calendar for upcoming gallery openings, and don't miss November's Día de los Muertos altar displays. (415-821-1155; www.missionculturalcenter.org; 2868 Mission St; 5-10pm Mon, from 10am Tue-Sat, 10am-5:30pm Sun; ; 14, 49, B 24th St Mission)

Eating

La Palma Mexicatessen

MEXICAN $

11 MAP P116, E7

Follow the applause: that's the sound of organic tortilla-making in progress. You've found the Mission mother lode of handmade tamales, and *pupusas* (tortilla pockets) with potato and *chicharones* (pork crackling), *carnitas* (slow-roasted pork), *cotija* (Oaxacan cheese) and La Palma's own tangy tomatillo sauce. Get takeout or bring a small army to finish the meal at sunny sidewalk tables. (📞415-647-1500; www.lapalmasf.com; 2884 24th St; tamales, tacos & huaraches $3-10; ⏰8am-6pm Mon-Sat, to 5pm Sun; 🚲; 🚌12, 14, 27, 48, Ⓑ24th St Mission)

Mr Pollo

INTERNATIONAL $

12 MAP P116, C7

This hole-in-the-wall restaurant contains just six tables and serves one of the most delicious, but least expensive, tasting menus in all of San Francisco. Vegetarians or anyone fussy should skip it, as the four always-changing courses are often heavy on meat. But adventurous omnivores will fully appreciate the artful cuisine, prepared with seasonal ingredients and inspired by the chef's travels. (2823 Mission St; four-course tasting menu $30; ⏰6-10pm Mon-Sat; 🚌12, 14, 48, 49, Ⓑ24th St Mission)

Mission Community Market

Back-alley bounty brings ravenous crowds on Thursdays to this nonprofit, neighborhood-run **market** (Map p116, C6; http://missioncommunitymarket. org; Bartlett St, btwn 21st & 22nd Sts; ⏰4-8pm Thu mid-Feb–mid-Nov; 🚲👶; 🚌14, 48, 49, Ⓑ24th St Mission), come rain or shine. More than 30 local farmers and food artisans offer California produce and inspired SF street food – look for Coastside Farms' smoked albacore, Far West Fungi's mushrooms, Flour Chylde pastries and Izalco Catering's *pupusas*. Enjoy shade, seating and mariachis at mural-lined La Placita.

Mission Cheese

CHEESE $

13 MAP P116, B4

Smile and say 'wine' at this cheese bar serving sublime pairings with expert advice and zero pretension. The all-domestic cheese menu ranges from triple creamy to extra stinky, raw cow's milk to sheep's milk, and California wines reign supreme. When in dairy doubt, try 'mongers choice' surprise cheese platters with pickles, nuts and dried fruit. (📞415-553-8667; www. missioncheese.net; 736 Valencia St; cheese flights $14; ⏰11am-9pm Tue-Thu & Sun, to 10pm Fri & Sat; 🚲; 🚌14, 22, 33, 49, 🚃J, Ⓑ16th St Mission)

Dessert in the Dogpatch

After you've pounded the pavement along the Dogpatch's sunny industrial waterfront or toured its one-of-a-kind **Museum of Craft & Design** (📞415-773-0303; www.sfmcd.org; 2569 3rd St; adult/student $8/6; ⏱11am-6pm Tue-Sat, noon-5pm Sun; 🚌22, 48, Ⓜ️T), you've pretty much earned a treat. Here's the good news: this neighborhood just happens to be San Francisco's sweet spot.

Mr & Mrs Miscellaneous (📞415-970-0750; 699 22nd St; ice cream $4-8; ⏱11:30am-6pm Wed-Sat, to 5pm Sun; 🚌22, 48, Ⓜ️T) factory-outlet ice-cream parlor does a brisk business in bourbon-caramel ice cream, while chocolatier **Michael Recchiuti** (📞415-489-2881; www.recchiuti.com; 801 22nd St; ⏱noon-7pm Mon-Fri, 11am-6pm Sat, noon-5pm Sun; 🚌22, 48, Ⓜ️T) concocts experimental candy in the Dogpatch before launching it at the Ferry Building (p54).

Craftsman & Wolves

BAKERY $

14 🍴 MAP P116, B4

Breakfast routines are made to be broken by the infamous Rebel Within: a sausage-spiked Asiago-cheese muffin with a silken soft-boiled egg baked inside. SF's surest pick-me-up is a Bellwether latte with *matcha* (green tea) cookies; stone yuzu coconut cakes and concoctions of sesame praline, passion fruit and vanilla creme are ideal for celebrating un-birthdays and imaginary holidays. (📞415-913-7713; www.craftsman-wolves.com; 746 Valencia St; pastries $3-16; ⏱6am-5pm Mon-Fri, from 8am Sat & Sun; 🚌14, 22, 33, 49, Ⓑ16th St Mission, Ⓜ️J)

Al's Place

CALIFORNIAN $$

15 🍴 MAP P116, C8

The Golden State dazzles on Al's plates, featuring homegrown heirloom ingredients, pristine Pacific seafood and grass-fed meat. Painstaking preparation yields sun-drenched flavors and exquisite textures: crispy-skin cod with frothy preserved-lime dip, and grilled peach melting into velvety foie gras. Dishes are half the size but thrice the flavor of mains elsewhere – get two or three and you'll be California dreaming. (📞415-416-6136; www.alsplacesf.com; 1499 Valencia St; share plates $15-21; ⏱5:30-10pm Wed-Sun; 🍴; 🚌12, 14, 49, Ⓜ️J, Ⓑ24th St Mission)

Tartine Manufactory

CALIFORNIAN $$

16 🍴 MAP P116, E4

What began as a baking power-house has evolved into a veritable smorgasbord of delicious, col-laborative, artisanal everything, set within an expansive yet deeply Instagram-worthy space appointed in light wood and exposed concrete. Need your morning caffeine fix? The Manufactory has its own coffee brand. Looking for a grab-and-go pastry? A sit-down breakfast? A lazy weekend brunch? Done, done and done. (📞415-757-0007; www. tartinemanufactory.com; 595 Alabama St; mains $16-38; ⏱8am-10pm; 🍴; 🚌12, 22, 27, 33)

Californios

LATIN AMERICAN $$$

17 ⓧ MAP P116, D6

Parades – from Carnaval to Día de los Muertos – are a Mission specialty, and the parade of Latin-inspired flavors nightly at Californios does justice to the neighborhood's roots and unbridled creativity. Chef Val Cantu collaborates with local farms and artisan producers to reinvent

staples with the seasons: imagine sourdough tortillas, foie-gras tamales, Dungeness crab ceviche and wild-strawberry flan. Reserve ahead. (📞415-757-0994; www. californiossf.com; 3115 22nd St; 16-course tasting menu $197; ⏱5:30-8:30pm Tue-Thu, to 9pm Fri & Sat; 🚌12, 14, 49, Ⓑ24th St Mission)

Foreign Cinema

CALIFORNIAN $$$

18 ⓧ MAP P116, C6

Chef Gayle Pirie's acclaimed California classics such as grilled Monterey calamari and crisp sesame fried chicken are the star attractions here – but subtitled films by Luis Buñuel and François Truffaut screening in the courtyard are mighty handy when conversation lags with first dates or in-laws. Get the red-carpet

Bi-Rite Creamery (p115)

Artistic Escape: Potrero Hill

These days the emerging Potrero Flats district (also called 'SoMiss-Po,' for SoMa, Mission and Potrero) is an eye-catcher for its arts centers, avant-garde galleries and repurposed bus depot housing the **California College of the Arts** (Wattis Institute; ☑Wattis Institute 415-355-9670; www.wattis.org; 360 Kansas St; admission free; ☉during school sessions noon-6pm Tue-Sat; ☐10, 19, 22, 33) campus.

Head under the highway overpass to discover **SOMArts** (p118), a nonprofit community hub for creative thinking that hosts shows featuring edible murals, global street dance-offs and new meanings for old words supplied by the pop-up Bureau of Linguistical Reality. Just down the street, the **San Francisco Center for the Book** (☑415-906-6417; www.sfcb.org; 375 Rhode Island St; gallery free; ☉gallery 10am-5:30pm; ☐8, 10, 19, 22, 33) features shows of handmade pop-up books and matchbook-sized 'zines, plus workshops for making your own.

The **Catharine Clark Gallery** (Map p116, F2; ☑415-399-1439; www.cclarkgallery.com; 248 Utah St; admission free; ☉10:30am-5:30pm Tue-Fri, 11am-6pm Sat; ☐9, 10, 19, 22, 27, 33) instigates art revolutions with Masami Teraoka's monumental paintings of geisha superheroines fending off wayward priests, while the **Hosfelt Gallery** (Map p116, F3; ☑415-495-5454; http://hosfeltgallery.com; 260 Utah St; admission free; ☉10am-5:30pm Tue, Wed & Fri & Sat, 11am-7pm Thu; ☐9, 10, 22, 27, 33) mesmerizes visitors with Emil Lukas' drawings made by thousands of fly larvae dragging ink across paper. Meanwhile, collage artists at the **Jack Fischer Gallery** (Map p116, F2; ☑415-522-1178; www.jackfischergallery.com; 311 Potrero Ave; admission free; ☉11am-5:30pm Tue-Sat; ☐8, 9, 22, 27, 33) bring intriguing interior worlds to life inside a warehouse space off Hwy 101. Friendly art debates continue around the corner at **Thee Parkside** (☑415-252-1330; www.theeparkside.com; 1600 17th St; ☉11am-2am Mon-Sat, to 8pm Sun; ☐10, 19, 22), where bikers and art students converge for cheap drinks, parking-lot BBQ and vintage photo booth photo-ops. But once alt-rock and punk bands start playing at **Bottom of the Hill** (☑415-621-4455; www.bottomofthehill.com; 1233 17th St; $5-20; ☉shows generally 9pm Tue-Sat; ☐10, 19, 22), artistic differences are set aside and mosh-pit mayhem reigns supreme.

treatment with valet parking ($15) and a well-stocked oyster bar. (📞415-648-7600; www.foreign cinema.com; 2534 Mission St; mains $28-36; 🕐5:30-10pm Sun-Wed, to 11pm Thu-Sat, brunch 11am-2:30pm Sat & Sun; 🚌12, 14, 33, 48, 49, Ⓑ24th St Mission)

Drinking

Trick Dog

BAR

19 Ⓔ MAP P116, E5

Drink adventurously with ingenious cocktails inspired by local obsessions: San Francisco muralists, Chinese diners or conspiracy theories. Every six months, Trick Dog adopts a new theme and the menu changes – proof you can teach an old dog new tricks and improve on classics like the

Manhattan. Arrive early for bar stools or hit the mood-lit loft for high-concept bar bites. (📞415-471-2999; www.trickdogbar.com; 3010 20th St; 🕐3pm-2am; 🚌12, 14, 49)

Zeitgeist

BAR

20 Ⓔ MAP P116, B1

You've got two seconds flat to order from tough-gal barkeeps used to putting macho bikers in their place – but with 48 beers on draft, you're spoiled for choice. Epic afternoons unfold in the beer garden, with folks hanging out and smoking at long tables. SF's longest happy hour lasts 9am to 6pm weekdays. Cash only; no photos (read: no evidence). (📞415-255-7505; www.zeitgeistsf.com; 199 Valencia St; 🕐9am-2am; 🚌14, 22, 49, Ⓑ16th St Mission)

Desserts, Foreign Cinema (p123)

Jolene's
LESBIAN

21 MAP P116, D2

Between the neon sign announcing 'you are safe here' and the custom-made boob wallpaper, women and nonbinary regulars have taken up quasi-permanent residence at Jolene's. Femme-focused parties like UHaul, live music, performances and theme nights (queer prom, anybody?) make a scene - grab your Purple Vesper (Tanqueray, vodka, Cocchi Americano and blue pea-flower) and try to keep up. (415-913-7948; www.jolenessf.com; 2700 16th St; 4pm-2am Thu-Fri, from 11am Sat & Sun; 12, 22, 55, B16th Mission St)

Bon Voyage
COCKTAIL BAR

22 MAP P116, B3

So, imagine a 1950s traveler who sets out to experience Southeast Asia and Africa, picking up art and curios along the way. Now think about this traveler repatriating to Palm Springs in the 1970s and throwing massive parties involving a giant disco ball, Chinese food and innovative, exotic cocktails. (www.bonvoyagebar.com; 584 Valencia St; cocktails $9-15; bar 2pm-2am Mon-Fri, from noon Sat & Sun; kitchen from 5pm Mon-Fri, from noon Sat & Sun; 14, 22, 33, 49, B16th St Mission)

El Rio
CLUB

23 MAP P116, C8

Work it all out on the dance floor with SF's most down and funky crowd – the full rainbow spectrum of colorful characters is here to party. Highlights include Salsa Sunday, free oysters from 5:30pm Friday, Queeraoke Wednesdays, drag-star DJs, backyard bands and ping-pong. Expect knockout margaritas and shameless flirting on a patio that's seen it all since 1978. (415-282-3325; www.elriosf.com; 3158 Mission St; cover free-$10; 2pm-2am Mon-Sat, to midnight Sun; 12, 14, 27, 49, B24th St Mission)

20 Spot
WINE BAR

24 MAP P116, C5

Find your California mellow at this neighborhood wine lounge in an 1885 Victorian building. After decades as Force of Habit punk-record shop – note the vintage sign – this corner joint has earned the right to unwind with a glass of Berkeley's Donkey and Goat sparkling wine and not get any guff. Caution: oysters with pickled persimmon could become a habit. (415-624-3140; www.20spot.com; 3565 20th St; 5pm-11pm Mon-Thu, to 12:30am Fri & Sat; 14, 22, 33, B16th St Mission)

Dalva & Hideout
LOUNGE

25 MAP P116, B3

SF's best bars are distinguished not just by their drinks but by the conversations they inspire – by both measures Dalva is top-shelf. Over ice-cold mugs of Pliny the Elder or curious seasonal brews, patrons discuss indie flicks they just caught at the Roxie (p129). Meanwhile, in the backroom Hideout, Dolores Park gossip spills over Dirty Pigeons (mezcal, lime, grapefruit, gentian bitters). (📞415-252-7740; www.dalvasf.com; 3121 16th St; ⏲4pm-2am, Hideout from 7pm; 🚌14, 22, 33, 49, Ⓑ24th St Mission)

%ABV

COCKTAIL BAR

26 📍 MAP P116, B3

As kindred spirits will deduce from the name (the abbreviation for 'percent alcohol by volume'), this bar is backed by cocktail crafters who know their Rittenhouse rye from their Japanese malt whiskey. Top-notch hooch is served promptly and without pretension, including excellent Cali wine and beer, and original historically inspired cocktails like the Sutro Swizzle (Armagnac, grapefruit shrub, maraschino liqueur). (📞415-400-4748; www.overproofsf.com; 3174

16th St; ⏲2pm-2am; 🚌14, 22, Ⓑ16th St Mission, Ⓜ J)

Ritual Coffee Roasters

CAFE

27 📍 MAP P116, C6

Cults wish they inspired the same devotion as Ritual, where regulars solemnly queue for house-roasted cappuccino with ferns drawn in foam and specialty drip coffees with highly distinctive flavor profiles – descriptions comparing roasts to grapefruit peel or hazelnut aren't exaggerating. Electrical outlets are limited to encourage conversation, so you can eavesdrop on dates and political-protest plans. (📞415-641-1011; www.ritualroasters.com; 1026 Valencia St; ⏲6am-8pm Mon-Fri, from 7am Sat & Sun; 🚌14, 49, Ⓑ24th St Mission)

Foreign Cinema (p123)

ANTHONY PIDGEON / LONELY PLANET ©

Roxie Cinema

JOHN S LANDER / GETTY IMAGES ©

Entertainment

Alamo Drafthouse Cinema
CINEMA

28 ⭐ MAP P116, C5

The landmark 1932 New Mission cinema is restored to its original Timothy Pfleuger–designed art-deco glory, and it's on a mission to upgrade dinner-and-a-movie dates. Staff deliver cocktails, beer and pizza to your plush banquette seats while you enjoy premieres, cult revivals (especially Music Mondays) or SF favorites, from *Mrs Doubtfire* to *Dirty Harry* – sometimes followed by filmmaker Q&As. (☏415-549-5959; www. drafthouse.com/sf; 2550 Mission St; tickets $6-20; 🚇14, Ⓑ24th St Mission)

ODC Theater
DANCE

29 ⭐ MAP P116, D3

For 45 years ODC has been redefining dance with risky, raw performances and the sheer joy of movement. ODC's season runs from September to December, but its stage presents year-round shows featuring local and international artists. (Oberlin Dance Collective; ☏box office 415-863-9834, classes 415-549-8519; www.odctheater. org; 3153 17th St; drop-in classes from $15, shows $20-50; 🚇12, 14, 22, 33, 49, Ⓑ16th St Mission)

Brava Theater
THEATER

30 ⭐ MAP P116, F7

Brava's been producing women-run theater for 30-plus years, hosting acts from comedian Sandra Bernhard to V-day monologist Eve Ensler, and it's the nation's first company with a commitment to producing original works by women of color and LGBTIQ+ playwrights. Brava honors the Mission's Mexican heritage with music and dance celebrations, plus hand-painted show posters modeled after Mexican cinema billboards. (☏415-641-7657; www.brava.org; 2781 24th St; 🚇12, 27, 33, 48)

Brick & Mortar
LIVE MUSIC

31 ⭐ MAP P116, C1

Some bands are too outlandish for regular radio – to hear them, you need San Francisco's Brick & Mortar. The bill here has featured national acts from brass-band showcases to the US air-guitar championships, plus homegrown SF upstarts like post-punk Magic Bullet, ironic 'indie-rock avalanche' the Yellow Dress and psychedelically groovy Loco Tranquilo. (📞415-678-5099; www.brickandmortarmusic. com; 1710 Mission St; cover $10-20; 🚋14, 49, Ⓑ16th St Mission)

Roxie Cinema

CINEMA

32 ⭐ MAP P116, B3

This vintage 1909 cinema is a neighborhood nonprofit with an international reputation for distributing documentaries and showing controversial films banned elsewhere. Tickets to film-festival premieres, rare revivals and raucous Oscars telecasts sell out – buy them online – but if the main show's packed, discover riveting

documentaries in teensy next-door Little Roxy instead. No ads, plus personal introductions to every film. (📞415-863-1087; www.roxie.com; 3117 16th St; regular screening/matinee $12-13/10; 🚋14, 22, 33, 49, Ⓑ16th St Mission)

Marsh

THEATER

33 ⭐ MAP P116, C6

Choose your seat wisely: you may spend the evening on the edge of it. One-acts and monologues here involve the audience in the creative process, from comedian W Kamau Bell's riffs to live tapings of National Public Radio's *Philosophy Talk*. Sliding-scale pricing allows everyone to participate and a few reserved seats are sometimes available (tickets $55). (📞415-641-0235;

Marsh

Gentrification in the Mission

As you frolic around the Mission, popping into precious and pricey little boutiques and fueling up on $14 peanut-washed Bulleit Bourbon cocktails or $10 hand-whisked *matcha*, you may encounter a group of Hispanic residents and neighborhood activists chanting about stopping evictions. Or, you might see a group of scooters blocking a shuttle route for tech company employees, many of whom now call the Mission home.

Here's why: the arrival of these wealthy employees has jacked up housing costs in a neighborhood long populated by South and Central American immigrants living on minimum wage. The median household income in the Mission was $37,000 in 1990, and many of those households were filled with entire extended families. Now, lots of those homes are being bought up by big-name tech employees making four or five times that amount.

The neighborhood was already coveted for its flat streets, sunny weather, cultural cache and proximity to the freeway and public transport. And as new money comes into the Mission, along with fancy restaurants and shops, it's become even more desirable. Crime has become less of a problem. And certainly there are new economic opportunities here for those in a position to capitalize.

Today, **Valencia Street** offers some of the best food, shopping and people-watching in the city, and travelers flock to it for these reasons. But during your visit, do keep in mind that some of the Hispanic residents, whose families have been here for five decades, are still trying to get by on meager incomes from their 99-cent stores, bodegas and taco shops.

You can learn more about the neighborhood by studying the gorgeous murals and you can also show support for long-standing local businesses by grabbing an empanada at a place like **Chile Lindo** (Map p116, C3; ☎415-621-6108; www.chilelindo.com; 2944 16th St; empanadas $5-6; ⏰8am-4pm Mon-Fri, from 10am Sat; 🚌14, 22, 33, Ⓑ16th St Mission), or a handmade tamale at **La Palma Mexicatessen** (p121). Check in with **Calle 24 Latino Cultural District** (Map p116, C7; www.calle24sf.org/; 3250 24th St) about events that may be going on during your visit, and other ways to get involved.

www.themarsh.org; 1062 Valencia St; tickets $15-55; ⊘box office 10am-5pm Mon-Fri; 🚌12, 14, 48, 49, Ⓑ24th St Mission)

Shopping

Adobe Books & Backroom Gallery
BOOKS

34 🔒 MAP P116, D7

Wall-to-wall inspiration – just-released fiction, limited-edition art books, rare cookbooks, well-thumbed poetry – plus 'zine launch parties, comedy nights and art openings. Mingle with Mission characters debating all-time-greatest pulp-fiction covers and SF history (founder Andrew is a whiz) and see SF artists at the Backroom Gallery (well worth the walk to the back of the store) before they hit Whitney Biennials. (📞415-864-3936; www.adobebooks.com; 3130 24th St; ⊘noon-8pm Mon-Fri, from 11am Sat & Sun; 🚌12, 14, 48, 49, Ⓑ24th St Mission)

Community Thrift
CLOTHING

35 🔒 MAP P116, B3

When local collectors and retailers have too much of a good thing, they donate it to nonprofit Community Thrift, where proceeds go to 200-plus local charities – all the more reason to gloat over your $5 totem-pole teacup, $10 vintage windbreaker and $14 disco-era glitter romper. Donate your cast-offs (until 5pm daily) and show some love to the Community. (📞415-861-4910; www.communitythriftsf.org; 623

Valencia St; ⊘10am-6:30pm; 🚌14, 22, 33, 49, Ⓑ16th St Mission)

Baggu
FASHION & ACCESSORIES

36 🔒 MAP P116, C5

Plastic bags are banned in San Francisco, which is a perfect excuse to stock up on SF designer Baggu's reusable Ripstop nylon totes in bright colors and quirky prints: sharks, alpacas and, ay, Chihuahuas. They're durable, lightweight and crushable – totes fabulous. Striped canvas backpacks are destined for hauling Adobe Books, and little leather circle purses hold Mission **Litquake** (www.litquake.org; ⊘mid-Oct) essentials. (www.baggu.com; 911 Valencia St; ⊘noon-7pm Mon-Fri, from 11am Sat & Sun; 🚌12, 14, 33, 49, Ⓜ J)

Mission Comics & Art
COMICS, ART

37 🔒 MAP P116, C4

Heads will roll, fists will fly and furious vengeance will be wreaked inside this mild-mannered shop stocking big-name and indie comics. Staff picks range from marquee (*Walking Dead*, *Star Wars*) to niche (*Snotgirl*, *Head Lopper*); artists headlining signings and gallery shows here have included *Supergirl* writer Mariko Tamaki, *Ancestor* surrealist artist Matt Sheean and *New Yorker* constructivist cartoonist Roman Muradov. (📞415-695-1545; www.missioncomicsandart.com; 2250 Mission St; ⊘noon-8pm Mon, Tue & Thu-Sat, from 11am Wed, noon-6pm Sun; 🚌12, 14, 33, 49, Ⓑ16th St Mission)

Tigerlily Perfumery

PERFUME

38 🔒 MAP P116, C5

If you want to bottle San Francisco and take it home with you, you've come to the right place. Tigerlily stocks an intoxicating variety of local perfumers' creations, which will transport you from beach days to Barbary Coast nights. Options range from Yosh Han's California-sunbeam scent, appropriately called U4EAHH!, to Ikiryo's kinky, leather-bound Bad Omen. Check for in-person perfume events. (📞415-896-4665; www.tigerlilysf.com; 973 Valencia St; ⏰noon-6:30pm Mon-Fri, to 7pm Sat, noon-5pm Sun; 🚌14, 33, 49, 🅱24th St Mission)

Bi-Rite

FOOD & DRINKS

39 🔒 MAP P116, B4

Diamond counters can't compare to the foodie dazzle of Bi-Rite's sublime wall of local artisan chocolates, treasure boxes of organic fruit and California wine and cheese selections expertly curated by upbeat, knowledgeable staff. Step up to the altar-like deli counter to provision five-star Dolores Park picnics. An institution since 1940, Bi-Rite champions good food for all through its nonprofit 18 Reasons (p120). (📞415-241-9760; www.biritemarket.com; 3639 18th St; ⏰8am-9pm; 👶; 🚌14, 22, 33, 49, 🅱16th St Mission, 🅼J)

Community Thrift Store (p131)

SABRINA DALBESIO / LONELY PLANET ©

Needles & Pens

ARTS & CRAFTS

40 🔒 MAP P116, C6

This scrappy zine shop/how-to source/art gallery/publisher delivers inspiration to create your own artworks, zines and repurposed fashion statements. Nab limited-edition printings of Xara Thustra's manifesto *Friendship Between Artists Is an Equation of Love and Survival* and H Finn Cunningham's *Mental Health Cookbook* – plus alphabet buttons to pin your own credo onto a handmade messenger bag. (📞 415-872-9189; www. needles-pens.com; 1173 Valencia St; 🕐 noon-7pm; 🚌 14, 33, 49, Ⓑ 24th St Mission)

Gravel & Gold

HOMEWARES

41 🔒 MAP P116, C5

Get back to the land and in touch with California's roots without leaving sight of a Mission sidewalk. Gravel & Gold celebrates California's hippie homesteader movement with hand-printed smock-dresses, signature boob-print totes and wiggly stoner-striped throw pillows. It's homestead California-style with hand-thrown stoneware mugs, Risograph posters and rare books on '70s beach-shack architecture – plus DIY maker workshops (see website). (📞 415-552-0112; www. gravelandgold.com; 3266 21st St; 🕐 noon-7pm Mon-Sat, to 5pm Sun; 🚌 12, 14, 49, Ⓑ 24th St Mission)

Harvest Off Mission

CANNABIS

42 🔒 MAP P116, C8

This tidy Bernal Heights dispensary is tops for its 'farm-to-feeling' edibles, which include things like animal cookies, Black Ice and Pineapple Love Bombs. Also, it may or may not be a coincidence that the incomparable Mitchell's Ice Cream is right down the block. (📞 415-814-3272; www.harvestshop. com/harvest-off-mission-menu; 33 29th St; 🕐 10am-9pm; 🚌 14, 49, Ⓜ J, Ⓑ 24th St Mission)

Explore ⊕
The Castro

Rainbow flags wave their welcome to all in the world's premier LGBTIQ+ culture destination — club kids, career activists and sequined drag queens. Check the plaques on Castro sidewalks and notice whose footsteps you're walking in — Nobel Laureates and censored poets, civil-rights leaders and San Francisco's very own Empress.

The Short List

○ **Castro Theatre (p143)** *Catching a movie premiere, sing-along musical or drag show.*

○ **GLBT History Museum (p139)** *Time-traveling through 50 years in the Castro at America's first LGBTIQ+ museum.*

○ **Frances (p141)** *Feasting on Melissa Perello's renegade rustic cuisine.*

○ **Rainbow Honor Walk (p139)** *Seeing how far we've come along Castro sidewalks honoring LGBTIQ+ pioneers.*

○ **Harvey Milk's Camera Store (p139)** *Admiring the messages of civil rights leader Harvey Milk.*

Getting There & Around

Ⓜ K, L and M trains run beneath Market St to Castro Station. J trains travel from downtown along Church to 18th St and beyond.

Streetcar Vintage streetcars operate on the F-Market line, from Fisherman's Wharf to Castro St.

🚌 Buses 24 and 33 serve the Castro, but there may be long waits between runs.

Neighborhood Map on p138

Castro Theatre (p143) DORI CHRONICLES / SHUTTERSTOCK ©

Walking Tour 🥾

The History-Making Castro

Within a few years of moving into this quaint Victorian neighborhood in the 1970s, the Castro's out-and-proud community elected Harvey Milk as the nation's first openly gay official. When AIDS hit, the Castro wiped its tears and got to work, advocating interventions that saved lives worldwide. Today the little neighborhood under the giant rainbow flag is a global symbol of freedom.

Walk Facts

Start Harvey Milk Plaza
End Harvey Milk's Camera Store
Length 0.3 miles; 1 hour

❶ Harvey Milk Plaza

A huge, irrepressibly cheerful rainbow flag waves hello as you emerge from the Castro St Muni station into **Harvey Milk Plaza** (cnr Market & Castro Sts; Ⓜ Castro St). Notice the plaque honoring the Castro camera-store-owner who became America's first out gay official. Milk was assassinated, but the Castro keeps his legacy of civil rights and civic pride alive.

❷ Twin Peaks Tavern

A vintage neon rainbow proudly points to **Twin Peaks** (p141), the world's first gay bar with windows open to the street.

❸ LGBTIQ+ Giants

Watch your step on Castro St, or you might step on Virginia Woolf or James Baldwin without even realizing it. They're among the 28 pioneering LGBTIQ+ figures featured in bronze sidewalk plaques in the Castro's **Rainbow Honor Walk** (p139).

❹ Castro Theatre

At the deco-fabulous **Castro Theatre** (p143), show tunes on a Wurlitzer are overtures to silver-screen gems, sing-along musicals, independent cinema, and live-action drag versions of cult classics.

❺ Strut

On crowded Castro St today, you'd never guess how hauntingly empty it was during the AIDS epidemic. In 1982, nonprofit San Francisco AIDS Foundation was formed to take preventive action, and set global standards for humane care. Today it provides the Castro's now-thriving community with free and low-cost health and wellness services at **Strut** (☎ 415-437-3400; www.strutsf.org; 470 Castro St; ⊙ Mon & Sat 10am-6pm, Tue-Thu to 8pm; 🚌 24, 33, Ⓜ F, K, L, M).

❻ Pride

America's first LGBTIQ+ history museum, the **GLBT History Museum** (p139) captures proud moments and historic challenges: Harvey Milk's campaign literature, interviews with trailblazing bisexual author Gore Vidal, matchbooks from long-gone bathhouses, and 1950s penal codes banning homosexuality.

❼ Harvey Milk's Camera Store

This storefront may look familiar: it was once **Harvey Milk's Camera Store** (p139), as featured in the Academy Award–winning biopic *Milk*. At the time of research, there were reports that it may soon be turned into a national landmark.

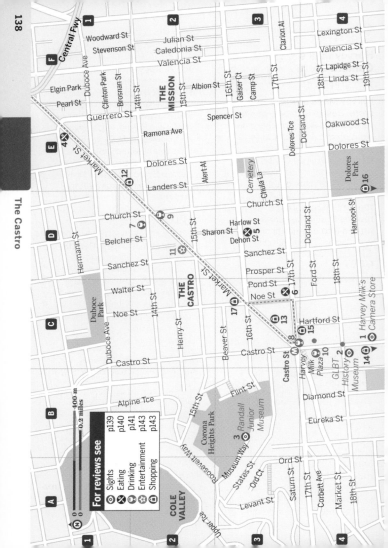

Central Fwy

Woodward St
Julian St
Stevenson St
Caledonia St
Valencia St

Lexington St
Clarion Al
Valencia St
Lapidge St
Linda St

Elgin Park
Clinton Park
Brosnan St
14th St
Albion St
Gaiser Ct
Camp St
17th St
18th St
19th St

Pearl St
Guerrero St

THE MISSION

15th St
16th St

Dorland St

Spencer St

Ramona Ave

Oakwood St

Market St

Dolores Tce

Dolores St

4

Dolores St
Alert Al
Chula La
Cemetery

Landers St

Dolores St

Dolores Park

16

12

Church St
Church St

9

Hermann St

Church St
Belcher St

7

Harlow St
Sharon St
Dehon St

5

Hancock St

11

Sanchez St
Prosper St
Pond St
Noe St

Ford St

Dorland St

18th St

Sanchez St
Walter St
Dubonce Park
Dubonce Ave

14th St

THE CASTRO

15th St
16th St

Henry St

17

6

Noe St

13

Hartford St

Harvey Milk's
Camera Store

Noe St
Castro St

Beaver St

Castro St

8

15

Harvey
Milk
Plaza

10

1

GLBT
History
Museum

2

14

Alpine Tce

15th St
Flint St

Randall
Junior
Museum

3

Diamond St

Eureka St

Dubonce Ave

Corona
Heights Park

Museum Way

Roosevelt Way

States St
Ord Ct

Ord St

Saturn St

Corbett Ave

Market St

17th St

18th St

COLE
VALLEY

Upper Tce

Levant St

For reviews see

◎	Sights	p139
✕	Eating	p140
◻	Drinking	p141
◻	Entertainment	p143
◻	Shopping	p143

400 m
0.2 miles

N

A   B   C   D   E   F

1   2   3   4

Sights

Harvey Milk's Camera Store
HISTORIC SITE

1 MAP P138, C4

Harvey Milk's former camera store, Castro Camera, was featured in the Academy Award–winning movie *Milk*, and for a time was home to the Human Rights Campaign Action Center, a civil-rights advocacy group championing marriage equality and transgender identity rights. At the time of research, there were reports that it may soon be turned into a national historic site. (575 Castro St; M Castro St)

GLBT History Museum
MUSEUM

2 MAP P138, C4

America's first gay history museum showcases a century's worth of San Francisco LGBTIQ+ ephemera – Harvey Milk's campaign literature, matchbooks from long-gone bathhouses, photographs of early marches – alongside insightful installations highlighting queer culture milestones and struggles for acceptance throughout history. Multimedia stories put civil rights efforts into personal perspective, and provide community introductions for queer folk and allies alike. The gift shop sells reproductions of '80s pink triangle tees, '70s pride pins, and Harvey Milk fridge magnets citing

Rainbow Honor Walk

You're always in excellent company in the Castro, where sidewalk plaques pay tribute to LGBTQI+ heroes. The **Rainbow Honor Walk** (http://rainbowhonorwalk.org; Castro St & Market St; M Castro St) runs along Market St from Noe St to Castro St and down Castro St from Market St to 20th St. Portraits are etched into the bronze plaques, and there are many familiar faces, including civil rights activist James Baldwin, artist Keith Haring, author Virginia Woolf, and disco diva Sylvester. Honorees are suitably bathed in glory every night, when they're illuminated by rainbow LEDs.

his words: 'You gotta give'em hope.' Indeed. (📞 415-621-1107; www.glbthistory.org/museum; 4127 18th St; $5, 1st Wed of month free; ⏱ 11am-6pm Mon-Sat, noon-5pm Sun, closed Tue fall-spring; M Castro St)

Randall Junior Museum
MUSEUM

3 MAP P138, B3

While adults are asleep downhill, eight-year-olds are making scientific discoveries atop **Corona Heights Park** (Museum Hill; btwn 16th St & Roosevelt Way; 🚌 37, M Castro St). After Josephine

Randall became a pioneering Stanford zoologist in 1910, she turned a jail into a kids' science and arts center as San Francisco's first Rec & Parks Superintendent. Today the kids' museum named after her features state-of-the-art science and tech labs, woodworking and ceramics studios. Highlights include a habitat for 100 stray and wounded animals, plus Lionel trains chugging along the Golden Gate Model Railroad. Check the website for wonder-inspiring hands-on workshops, often available on a walk-in basis. (☎ 415-554-9600; www.randall museum.org; 199 Museum Way; admission free; ⏱10am-5pm Tue-Sat; 🅿 🚻; 🚌 24, 37, Ⓜ F, K, L, M)

Eating

Kantine

SCANDINAVIAN $

4 🍴 MAP P138, E1

Brunch is served with a side of *hygge* (cozy happiness) at Kantine. Take your pick of five to seven seasonal Scandinavian-inspired dishes – velvety bay shrimp and egg salad, lemony pickled herring – or hearty *smør-rebrød* (open-faced sandwich) on nutty, toothsome, just-baked sprouted rye. Chef-owner Nichole Achettola turns local, sustainable, organic ingredients into decadent, curative, clean fare that honors Castro's Scandinavian heritage and Kantine's location in an ex-laundromat (love the laundry-bagged lights).(☎ 415-735-7123;

Seward Street Slides

www.kantinesf.com; 1906 Market St;
dishes $10-19; ⏲7:30am-3pm Tue-Fri,
from 9am Sat & Sun; 🚼👪; 🚍22,
Ⓜ F, J, K, L, M)

Gai Chicken Rice HAINAN $

5 🍴 MAP P138, D3

Who's got the solution to cold
snaps and tentative tummies?
This Gai. The tender Hainan-style
poached chicken here is free range
and antibiotic-free, accompanied
by jasmine or brown rice cooked
in chicken broth, with sweet-and-
sour cucumbers and your choice
of gingery Hainan, tangy Vietnamese, Thai soy or housemade
habanero sauces. Soulful soup
gets you back on your feet; sweet-
ened Vietnamese coffee gets you
Castro-club-hopping. (📞415-
0451; www.gaiandrice.com; 3463 16th
St; dishes $11-13; ⏲11:30am-8:30pm;
🚼👪; 🚍22, Ⓜ F, J, K, L, M)

Frances CALIFORNIAN $$$

6 🍴 MAP P138, C3

Rebel chef-owner Melissa Perello
earned a Michelin star for fine dining, then ditched downtown to start
this market-inspired neighborhood
bistro. Daily menus showcase rustic
flavors and luxurious textures with
impeccable technique – handmade
ricotta *malfatti* pasta with buttery
squash and crunchy pepitas, juicy
pork chops with blood orange and
earthy Japanese sweet potatoes –
plus cult wine served by the ounce,
directly from Wine Country. (📞415-
621-3870; www.frances-sf.com; 3870
17th St; mains $26-34; ⏲5-10pm Sun &

Seward Street Slides

Race ya! Twin concrete **slides**
(Seward St, cnr Douglass St;
⏲daylight hours; 👪; 🚍33, Ⓜ F,
K, L, M) snake down a steep
hill – it's an urban luge, built in
1973. Cardboard is necessary
for descents, and there's usually a stack by the slides – but
BYO waxed paper for faster
speeds.

Tue-Thu, to 10:30pm Fri & Sat; 🚍24, 33,
Ⓜ F, K, L, M)

Drinking

Last Rites TIKI BAR

7 🍸 MAP P138, D2

An airplane crashed on a desert
island, and out of the wreckage
came this killer Castro tiki bar.
Enter through the airplane door to
discover a long-lost jungle world,
where tattoo artists and software
engineers clink flaming rum drinks
over steamer-trunk tables. A giant
skull glowers from fern-covered
walls, daring you to finish that second Zombie Killer. Brace for impact.
(www.lastritesbar.com; 718 14th St;
⏲6pm-2am; 👪; 🚍22, Ⓜ F, J, K, L, M)

Twin Peaks Tavern LGBTIQ+

8 🍸 MAP P138, C3

The vintage rainbow neon sign
points the way to a local landmark
– Twin Peaks was the world's first
gay bar with windows open to the

LARA HATA / GETTY IMAGES ©

Bartender preparing martinis

street. If you're not here for the Castro's best people-watching, cozy up to the Victorian carved-wood bar for cocktails and conviviality, or grab a back booth to discuss movies at the Castro over wine by the glass. (📞415-864-9470; www.twinpeakstavern.com; 401 Castro St; 🕐noon-2am Mon-Fri, from 8am Sat & Sun; Ⓜ Castro St)

Verve Coffee Roasters

CAFE

9 🚇 MAP P138, D2

Cults wish they had the devoted following of this Santa Cruz roaster, justifiably worshipped for small-batch, single-origin roasts prepared with pride. Chipper baristas will ask if you want your milk microfoamed for denser consistency – say yes and tip in cash. Tasty breakfast biscuits and a sunny corner spot encourage people-watching – don't let the silent stressy laptop crowd kill your vibe. (📞415-780-0867; www.verve coffee.com; 2101 Market St; 🕐6am-8pm; 🚌22, Ⓜ F, J, K, L, M)

440 Castro

LGBTIQ+

10 🍸 MAP P138, C4

The most happening bar on the street, 440 Castro draws bearded, gym-fit 30- and 40-something dudes – especially on scruffy Sundays and weekend nights – and an odd mix of Peter Pans for Monday's underwear night. If you think the monthly Battle of the Bulge contest has something to do with WWII, this is not your bar.

(📞415-621-8732; www.the440.com; 440 Castro St; 🕐noon-2am; 🚇24, 33, Ⓜ F, K, L, M)

Entertainment

Swedish American Hall & Cafe du Nord

LIVE MUSIC

11 ⭐ MAP P138, D2

The Castro was once known as Little Scandinavia after the sailors who docked here – and the secret to their community spirit was the speakeasy running in the basement of their local meeting hall since 1907. Today the updated Cafe du Nord speakeasy is an atmospheric singer-songwriter hotspot, while shipshape upstairs Swedish American Hall hosts the bigger indie-breakthrough Noise Pop and folkYEAH! concert series. (📞415-375-3370; www.swedishamericanhall.com; 2170 Market St; shows $12-35; 🕐shows start 6:30-8pm; Ⓜ Church St)

Shopping

Apothecarium

CANNABIS

12 🔒 MAP P138, E1

What's that alluring frosted-glass emporium – the lovechild of an Apple Store and Victorian lingerie boutique? Just as you suspected: it's America's best-designed marijuana dispensary, according to *Architectural Digest*. For the full effect, consult staff about edibles for your desired state, from mellow to giddy – and then you can *really* appreciate the local art from designer couches. It's 18+ only; ID required. (📞415-500-2620; https://apothecarium.com; 2029 Market St; 🕐9am-9pm; 🚇22, 37, Ⓜ F, J, K, L, M)

Stag & Manor

HOMEWARES, DESIGN

13 🔒 MAP P138, C3

Dashingly handsome decor from indie design boutique Stag & Manor lets you take the Castro home. Macrame wall hangings give

---

Castro Theatre

Every night at the **Castro** (Map p138, C4; 📞415-621-6120; www.castrotheatre.com; 429 Castro St; adult $13, child, senior & matinee $10; Ⓜ Castro St), crowds roar as the mighty organ rises – and no, that's not a euphemism. Showtime at this 1922 art-deco movie palace is heralded with Wurlitzer organ show tunes, culminating in singalongs to the Judy Garland anthem 'San Francisco.' The theater's neon marquee announces upcoming features, including silver-screen classics and film festival premieres. But check the website to score tickets to wildly popular drag reenactments of cult flicks – from *Valley of the Dolls* to *Mean Girls* – and sing-along musicals. It's quintessential San Francisco, and a cinema experience like no other.

your pad California creds, brass-ball lanterns wink welcome at your guests, and minimalist fair-trade throw pillows hint to dates that you're thoughtful, laid-back, and well-traveled. Well-priced, globally minded, and neighbor-owned – friendly Castro owner Seth Morrison is here to solve design dilemmas. (📞415-997-8241; https://stagandmanor.com; 2327 Market St; ⏰noon-7pm Tue-Thu & Sat, to 5pm Fri & Sun; 🚃24, 33, Ⓜ F, J, K, L, M)

Charlie's Corner

BOOKS

14 🔒 MAP P138, C4

For Castro kids, the biggest neighborhood attraction is over the hill at Charlie's Corner, a storybook world where kids are invited to read, draw and sing along. This bookstore is a magical forest,

where kids gather around a tree and sit on toadstools for story hours four times daily in English, Spanish and French – sometimes with live music and art projects. (📞415-641-1104; https://charliescorner.com; 4102 24th St; ⏰9:30am-6pm Mon-Fri, 10am-5pm Sat & Sun; 🚶; 🚃24, 48, Ⓜ J)

Local Take

GIFTS & SOUVENIRS

15 🔒 MAP P138, C4

Take in the local scenery at Local Take, a gallery of original SF souvenirs made and designed by locals. Bring home your very own Castro landmark – like a Castro Theatre marquee print, Sutro Tower tote, F Castro streetcar T-shirt or belt buckle featuring vintage Muni maps – and support SF's creative economy. Check online for events

Twin Peaks Tavern (p141) at Castro and 17th Streets

Community Bulletins

Newspaper If you don't spot a copy of the LBGTIQ+ *Bay Area Reporter* newspaper in Castro bookstores and cafes, check out the community's newspaper of record since 1971 at www.ebar.com.

Notice board To see what's happening in the Castro now, check out the outdoor bulletin board behind the **Walgreens** (☎ 415-861-3136; www.walgreens.com; 498 Castro St, cnr 18th St; ⏱ 24hr; 🚌 24, 33, 35, Ⓜ F, K, L, M) at 18th and Castro – circuit parties, lost cats, drag shows, missed connections, parenting support groups, bands seeking lead guitarists.

Altars Across rainbow crosswalks at 18th and Castro, you may spot impromptu altars with glitter, candles, flowers and notes honoring friends of the community who have died or are celebrating a landmark achievement – always a touching sight.

with local makers. (☎ 415-556-5300; http://localtakesf.com; 3979b 17th St; ⏱ 11am-7pm; 🚌 24, 33, Ⓜ F, K, L, M)

Omnivore

BOOKS

16 🔒 MAP P138, E4

Salivate over signed cookbooks by chef-legend Alice Waters and signed first editions of Berkeley chef Samin Nosrat's *Salt Fat Acid Heat*, and stay for standing-room-only in-store events with star chefs and food luminaries like Michael Pollan. Satisfy insatiable appetites with specialty titles covering ancient Filipino diets, Lebanese preservation methods, and DIY moonshine. Don't miss vintage cookbooks and ephemera like antique absinthe labels. (☎ 415-282-4712; www.omnivorebooks.com; 3885a Cesar Chavez St; ⏱ 11am-6pm Mon-Sat, noon-5pm Sun; Ⓜ J)

Castro Farmers Market

MARKET

17 🔒 MAP P138, C3

Find local and organic produce and artisan foods at moderate prices, plus charmingly offbeat folk music March through December. (www.pcfma.com; Noe St, cnr Market St; ⏱ 4-8pm Wed Mar-Dec; Ⓜ Castro St)

Explore
The Haight &
Hayes Valley

Hippie idealism lives in the Haight, with street musicians, anarchist comic books and psychedelic murals galore. Browse local designs and go gourmet in Hayes Valley, where Zen monks and jazz legends drift down the sidewalks.

The Short List

○ **Haight St (p148)** *Bringing back the Summer of Love with flowers and freestyle folk songs.*

○ **SFJAZZ (p158)** *Toasting jazz giants between sets in front of Sandow Birk's tiled music-history mural.*

○ **Alamo Square Park (p154)** *Admiring Victorian mansions that have hosted earthquake refugees, speakeasies and satanic rites.*

○ **Haight Street Art Center (p154)** *Finding inspiration at poster art shows and spotting the hidden WPA mural.*

○ **Bound Together Anarchist Book Collective (p161)** *Perusing prison lit and radical comics at this volunteer-run outpost of Left Coast ideas.*

Getting There & Around

🚌 Bus routes 5, 6, 7, 21, 22, 24, 33, 37 & 43 serve this neighborhood.

Streetcar The N line offers a shortcut from downtown and the Lower Haight to the Upper Haight, and onward to Ocean Beach.

Ⓑ Civic Center BART station is four blocks east of Hayes Valley.

Neighborhood Map on p152

Haight neighborhood

Top Experience 📷
Revisit the '60s on Haight Street

Was it the fall of 1966 or the winter of '67? As the saying goes, if you can remember the Summer of Love, you probably weren't there. The fog was laced with pot, sandalwood incense and burning draft cards, and the corner of Haight and Ashbury Sts became the turning point for nonconformists dubbed 'hippies.'

◎ MAP P152, G5

btwn Central & Stanyan Sts

🚌 7, 22, 33, 43, Ⓜ N

Feel the Flower Power

Hippie tie-dyes and ideals have never entirely gone out of fashion in the Haight – hence the prized vintage rock tees on the wall at Wasteland (p161) and organic-farming manuals in their umpteenth printing at Bound Together Anarchist Book Collective (p161). To see where rock-star residents lived and loved freely, take a self-guided Flashback Walking Tour (p150).

Flashbacks are a given in the Haight, where the fog is fragrant downwind of Haight St's legal marijuana dispensaries. You'll notice the clock on the northeast corner of Haight and Ashbury reads 4:20 – a term coined in the Bay Area circa 1971, now recognized globally as a reference to International Bong Hit time. Recently, a local clockmaker took it upon himself to get the vintage clock running again. Within days, stoned pranksters reset it to 4:20.

Since the '60s, bad trips and unfortunate itches have been mercifully treated gratis at the **Haight-Ashbury Free Clinic** (HealthRIGHT 360; 415-746-1950; www.healthright360.org; 558 Clayton St; by appointment 8:45am-noon & 1-5pm; 6, 7, 33, 37, 43, M N). From the same era, Haight St has separated into two camps, divided by the Divisadero St strip of indie boutiques, trendy bars and restaurants now called **NoPa** (North of the Panhandle). The **Upper Haight** specializes in potent coffee, radical literature and retail therapy for rebels, while the **Lower Haight** has better beer selections and fantastic rock art openings at Haight Street Art Center (p154) and Family Affair (p154).

★ Top Tips

• Panhandling has been part of the Upper Haight scene since the '60s, from busking street musicians to teen runaways scrounging for bus fare home.

• The Lower Haight is more low-key, though the mellow vibes are occasionally disrupted by petty crime northeast of Fillmore and Haight Sts.

✗ Take a Break

Magnolia Brewery (415-864-7468; www.magnoliapub.com; 1398 Haight St; mains $14-26; 11am-10pm Mon-Thu, to 11pm Fri, 10am-11pm Sat, to 10pm Sun; 6, 7, 33, 43) serves beer samplers with house-made sausages.

Walking Tour 🥾

Haight Flashback

A walk in the Haight is a step back in time, and will likely involve hippies reminiscing about glory days (trailed by teenage relations pretending not to know them). Other highlights include groovy green spaces, rock-star crash pads and a radical rehab center.

Walk Facts

Start Buena Vista Park
End Golden Gate Park
Length 1.3 miles; one hour

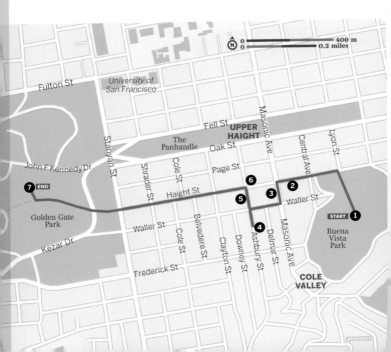

❶ Buena Vista Park

Start in **Buena Vista Park** (http://sfrecpark.org; Haight St, btwn Central Ave & Baker St; ☉sunrise-sunset; 🐾; 🚌6, 7, 37, 43), with panoramic city views that moved San Franciscans to tears after the 1906 earthquake. Founded in 1867, this is one of the oldest city parks – and it's ringed by century-old California oaks.

❷ Bound Together Anarchist Book Collective

Heading west up Haight St, you may recognize Emma Goldman in the *Anarchists of the Americas* mural at **Bound Together Anarchist Book Collective** (p161) – if not, staff can recommend biographical comics by way of introduction.

❸ 1235 Masonic Ave

Neighborhood old-timers claim the Symbionese Liberation Army used 1235 Masonic Ave as a safe house for kidnapped-heiress-turned-revolutionary-bank-robber Patty Hearst. To live here now, you'd have to rob a bank – a one-bedroom apartment recently sold for $1.5 million.

❹ Grateful Dead House

Turn right onto Waller St and left uphill past 32 Delmar St, site of the Sid Vicious overdose that broke up the Sex Pistols in 1978. A block over, pay your respects to Jerry Garcia, Bob Weir and Pigpen at the **Grateful Dead House** (p155), site of the band's 1967 drug bust – and landmark press conference demanding the decriminalization of marijuana. Fifty years later, the state of California complied.

❺ 635 Ashbury St

Down the block, 635 Ashbury St is one of many known SF addresses for Janis Joplin, who had a hard time hanging onto leases in the 1960s – but as she sang, 'Freedom's just another word for nothin' left to lose.'

❻ Haight-Ashbury Free Clinic

At the corner of Haight and Ashbury, the clock overhead always reads 4:20, better known in 'Hashbury' as International Bong-Hit Time. For trips gone bad, **Haight-Ashbury Free Clinic** (p149) offered free recovery treatment and still provides care to all. You'll spot its hand-carved 1967 sign at the corner of Cole and Haight, below its motto: 'Healthcare is a right, not a privilege – love needs care.'

❼ Hippie Hill

Cross Haight and Cole Sts, and across the street from the apartment where Charles Manson once lived, you'll spot a Summer of Love relic: Joana Zegri's 1967 **Evolutionary Rainbow** mural. Once a shop owner painted it over – and faced community boycotts until it was restored. Follow your bliss to the drum circle at Hippie Hill in **Golden Gate Park** (p164), where free spirits have gathered since the '60s to flail to the beat.

A B Turk St C D

WESTERN
Elm St ADDITION Golden Gate Ave

1

Seymour St

Scott St

Pierce St

Steiner St

Fillmore St

McAllister St

⊗ 8

NOPA

Fulton St

2

⊗ 6

Grove St

Grove St

Alamo
2 ⊙ Square
Park

Hayes St

19 ☆

14 ◉

3

Hayes St

◉ 12

Fell St

Pierce St

Scott St

Broderick St

Divisadero St

**LOWER
HAIGHT**

4

**UPPER
HAIGHT**

Page St

Pierce St

Steiner St

Fillmore St

◉ 13

Laussat St

Upper Haight
(0.2mi; see inset)
←

◉ Family
3 Affair

Walter St

Potomac St

Germania St

5

Buena
Vista
Park

Hermann St

For reviews see	
⊙ Top Experiences	p148
◉ Sights	p154
⊗ Eating	p155
◉ Drinking	p157
☆ Entertainment	p158
🔒 Shopping	p161

Lloyd St

Duboce
Park

Duboce Ave

Noe St

Walter St

**THE
CASTRO**

6

Ⓝ 0 ─────── 400 m
0 ─────── 0.2 miles

A B C D

McAllister St

11
Ash St

Fulton St

**CIVIC
CENTER**

1

McAllister St

Laguna St

Fulton St

Birch St

Grove St

Grove St

Gough St

Franklin St

Webster St

Buchanan St

Ivy St

Octavia St

Hayes St

2

Patricia's
Green

22

Linden St

17

9

23

Fell St

Linden St

Hickory St

Fell St

**HAYES
VALLEY**

Octavia St

Oak St

5

Hickory St

Oak St

7

3

Octavia Blvd

Lily St

Webster St

Lily St

Page St

Buchanan St

Laguna St

Page St

Zen
Center

Rose St

10

Brady St

Page St

Rose St

Octavia St

Market St

Gough St

4

Haight St

Laguna St

Waller St

16 Valencia St

Laussat St

Buchanan St

1
Haight
Street Art
Center

Upper Haight

Page St

Ashbury St

See Main Map
(0.2mi)

Page St

Cole St

24 18

*Haight
Street*

Haight St

Masonic Ave

5

21

Shrader St

15

Clayton St

20

UPPER
HAIGHT

Cole St

Belvedere St

Waller St

Delmar St

*Amoeba
Music*

*Grateful
Dead
House*

4

Waller St

Cole St

Downey St

**COLE
VALLEY**

6

0 —————— 200 m
0 —————— 0.1 miles

Sights

Haight Street Art Center

ARTS CENTER

 1 MAP P152, F4

Jeremy Fish's bronze bunny-skull sculpture hints at the weird wonders inside this nonprofit dedicated to works on paper and San Francisco's signature art form: screen-printed posters. Glimpse rock-concert posters currently in progress at the on-site screen-printing studio, plus jaw-dropping gallery shows, which have included Ralph Steadman's original illustrations for Hunter S Thompson's *Fear and Loathing in Las Vegas*. Gracing the stairwell is a hidden SF treasure: Ruben Kaddish's 1937 WPA fresco *Dissertation on Alchemy*, surely the trippiest mural ever commissioned by the US government. (📞415-363-6150; https://haightstreetart.org; 215 Haight St; admission free; ⏱noon-6pm Wed-Sun; 🚌6, 7, 22, Ⓜ F)

Alamo Square Park

PARK

2 MAP P152, C3

Hippie communes and Victorian bordellos, jazz greats and opera stars, earthquakes and Church of Satan services: these genteel 'Painted Lady' Victorian mansions have hosted them all since 1857, and survived elegantly intact. Pastel 'Postcard Row' mansions (aka the *Full House* sitcom backdrop) along the southeastern edge of this hilltop park pale in comparison

Zen Center

With its sunny courtyard and generous cased windows, this uplifting 1922 **building** (Map p152, F4; 📞415-863-3136; http://sfzc.org; 300 Page St; ⏱9:30am-12:30pm & 1:30-4pm Mon-Fri, 8:30am-noon Sat; bookstore 1:30-5:30pm & 6:30-7:30pm Mon-Thu, 1:30-5:30pm Fri, 11am-1pm Sat; 🚌6, 7, 21, 22) is an interfaith landmark. Since 1969 it's been home to the largest Buddhist community outside Asia. Before she built Hearst Castle, Julia Morgan (California's first licensed woman architect) designed this Italianate brick structure to house the Emanu-El Sisterhood, a residence for low-income Jewish working women.

with the colorful, turreted, outrageously ornamented Queen Anne Victorians along the northwestern end. (www.sfparksalliance.org/our-parks/parks/alamo-square; cnr Hayes & Steiner Sts; ⏱sunrise-sunset; 🚼; 🚌5, 21, 22, 24)

Family Affair

GALLERY

3 MAP P152, C5

Can you see sound? The answer is always yes at this music-inspired art gallery, named for the anthem by SF soul supergroup Sly and the Family Stone. Past synesthesia-inducing shows include video art illustrating DJ J

Dilla's sonic collages, lost album art by Bay Area hip-hop legends, and photographs of Prince, taken before he was famous, by his Bay Area producer. (📞415-757-0670; www.facebook.com/FamilyAffairHQ; 683 Haight St; admission free; 🕑noon-7pm Wed-Sat; 🚌6, 7, 22, 24)

Grateful Dead House
NOTABLE BUILDING

4 ◉ MAP P152, G6

Like surviving members of the Grateful Dead, this purple Victorian sports a touch of gray – but during the Summer of Love, this was where Jerry Garcia and bandmates blew minds, amps and brain cells. After they were busted for drugs in 1967, the Dead held a press conference here arguing for decriminalization. They claimed if everyone who smoked marijuana were arrested, San Francisco would be empty. Point taken, eventually – in 2016, California legalized adult recreational marijuana use in private (read: not the sidewalk, dude). (710 Ashbury St; 🚌6, 7, 33, 37, 43)

Eating

RT Rotisserie
CALIFORNIAN $

5 🍴 MAP P152, H3

An all-star menu makes ordering mains easy – you'll find bliss with entire chickens hot off the spit, succulent lamb and pickled onions, or surprisingly decadent roast cauliflower with earthy beet-tahini sauce – but do you choose porcini-powdered fries or signature salad with that? A counter staffer calls it: 'Look, I don't normally go for salads, but this one's next-level.' So true. No reservations. (www.rtrotisserie.com; 101 Oak St; dishes $9-14; 🕑11am-9pm; 🥗👶; 🚌5, 6, 7, 21, 47, 49, Ⓜ Van Ness)

The Mill
BAKERY $

6 🍴 MAP P152, A2

Baked with organic wholegrain flour stone-ground on-site, hearty Josey Baker Bread sustains Haight skaters and start-uppers alike. You might think SF hipsters are gullible for queuing for pricey toast, until you taste the truth: slathered in housemade hazelnut spread or California-grown almond butter, it's a proper meal. Housemade granola with Sonoma yogurt starts SF days right, and hearty seasonal sandwiches fuel Alamo Sq hikes. (📞415-345-1953; www.themillsf.com; 736 Divisadero St; toast $4-7; 🕑7am-9pm; 🥗👶; 🚌5, 21, 24, 38)

Rich Table
CALIFORNIAN $$

7 🍴 MAP P152, G3

Impossible cravings begin at Rich Table, where mind-bending dishes like porcini doughnuts, sardine chips, and *burrata* (cheese made from mozzarella and cream) funnel cake blow up Instagram feeds nightly. Married co-chefs and owners Sarah and Evan Rich riff on seasonal San Francisco cuisine with the soul of SFJAZZ stars and the ingenuity of Silicon

Valley regulars. (📞415-355-9085; http://richtablesf.com; 199 Gough St; mains \$17-37; 🕙5:30-10pm Sun-Thu, to 10:30pm Fri & Sat; 🚌5, 6, 7, 21, 47, 49, Ⓜ Van Ness)

Brenda's Meat & Three SOUTHERN US \$\$

8 🍴 MAP P152, A2

The name means one meaty main course plus three sides – though only superheroes finish ham steak with Creole red-eye gravy and exemplary grits, let alone cream biscuits and eggs. Chef Brenda Buenviaje's portions are defiantly Southern, which explains brunch lines of marathoners and partyers who forgot to eat last night. Arrive early, share sweet-potato pancakes, and pray for crawfish

Madrone Art Bar

CANNON PHOTOGRAPHY LLC / ALAMY STOCK PHOTO ©

specials. (📞415-926-8657; http://brendasmeatandthree.com; 919 Divisadero St; mains \$9-20; 🕙8am-10pm Wed-Mon; 🚌5, 21, 24, 38)

Petit Crenn CALIFORNIAN, FRENCH \$\$\$

9 🍴 MAP P152, F2

Leave gimmicky waterfront bistros behind and find higher ground here, with rustic French seafood and easy social graces. Triple-Michelin-starred chef Dominique Crenn offers a Brittany-inspired tasting menu nightly – items change seasonally, but include standout canapés (puffy *gougères* – cheese choux pastries – will haunt your dreams) and inspired coastal dishes like truffled steelhead and pistachio-oiled sea urchin. Reservations and prepayment required; meal price includes service. (📞415-864-1744; www.petitcrenn.com; 609 Hayes St; dinner tasting menu \$95, brunch mains \$15-24; 🕙5-9:30pm Tue-Thu, 11am-2pm & 5-9:30pm Sat, 11am-2pm & 5-9pm Sun; 🚌5, 21)

Zuni Cafe AMERICAN \$\$\$

10 🍴 MAP P152, H4

Gimmickry is for amateurs – Zuni has been turning basic menu staples into gourmet go-tos since 1979. Reservations and fat wallets are key for oyster-and-martini lunches, but the see-and-be-seen seating is a kick and the local, sustainably sourced signatures beyond reproach: Caesar salad with house-cured anchovies, brick-oven-roasted free-range chicken with Tuscan bread salad, and mesquite-grilled, grass-fed-beef burgers on focaccia (shoestring fries $9 extra). (☎ 415-552-2522; www.zunicafe.com; 1658 Market St; mains $15-33; ⏰ 11:30am-11pm Tue-Thu, to midnight Fri & Sat, 11am-11pm Sun; 🚌 6, 7, 47, 49, Ⓜ Van Ness)

Drinking

Smuggler's Cove BAR

11 🔵 MAP P152, G1

Yo-ho-ho and a bottle of rum... wait, make that a Dead Reckoning (Nicaraguan rum, port, pineapple, bitters), unless you'll split the flaming Scorpion Bowl? Pirates are bedeviled by choice at this Barbary Coast–shipwreck tiki bar, hidden behind tinted-glass doors. With 550 rums and 70-plus cocktails gleaned from rum-running around the world – and $2 off 5pm to 6pm daily – you won't be dry-docked long. (☎ 415-869-1900; www. smugglerscovesf.com; 650 Gough St; ⏰ 5pm-1:15am; 🚌 5, 21, 47, 49, Ⓜ Civic Center, Ⓑ Civic Center)

Madrone Art Bar BAR

12 🔵 MAP P152, B3

Drinking becomes an art form at this Victorian parlor crammed with graffiti installations and absinthe fountains. Motown Mondays feature the Ike Turner drink special – Hennessy served with a slap – but nothing beats the monthly Prince/Michael Jackson throw-down dance party. Performers redefine genres: punk-grass (bluegrass

Smuggler's Cove

and punk), blunt-funk (reggae and soul) and church, no chaser (Sunday-morning jazz organ). Cash only. (☎ 415-241-0202; www. madroneartbar.com; 500 Divisadero St; cover free-$5; ⏰ 4pm-2am Tue-Sat, 3pm-1:30am Sun; 🚌 5, 6, 7, 21, 24)

Noc Noc BAR

13 🔵 MAP P152, D4

Who's there? Steampunk blacksmiths, anarchist hackers, trance DJs practicing for Burning Man, and other San Francisco characters straight out of an R Crumb comic, that's who. Happy hour lasts until 7pm daily with $4 local drafts (no PBR here), and hot sake is $1 after 10pm – but mixing black-and-tans with potent house sake will Noc-knock you off your junkyard-art stool. (☎415-861-5811; www.nocnocs.com; 557 Haight St; ⏰5pm-2am Mon-Thu, from 3:30pm Fri, from 3pm Sat & Sun; 🚌6, 7, 22, 24, Ⓜ N)

Emporium ARCADE, BAR

14 🚇 MAP P152, A3

Game on, gamers – this former movie palace is an adult playground with full bar, video games, billiards, air hockey and themed pinball. Beat Dirty Harry at his own game, or curse in Klingon over *Star Trek: The Next Generation* game. Check website for weekend DJ lineups and open hours – Emporium gets booked for tech industry events. Bring ID; 21+ only. (https:// emporiumsf.com; 616 Divisadero St; ⏰4pm-2am Mon-Fri, 2pm-2am Sat & Sun; 🚌5, 21, 24)

Alembic BAR

15 🚇 MAP P152, F5

The Victorian tin ceilings are hammered, and you could be too unless you sip these potent concoctions slowly – all expertly crafted from 250 specialty spirits. Classics include the newfangled old fashioned with brown-butter bourbon, but the seasonal menu features limited-edition wonders like summer's Swizzle Me This (gin, rum, black pepper, strawberry, Angostura bitters) and winter's Warm Core (citrus, pickled pineapple, Brugal 188 rum float). (☎415-666-0822; www.alembicbar. com; 1725 Haight St; ⏰4pm-midnight Tue & Wed, to 2am Thu & Fri, 11am-2am

Sat, 11am-midnight Sun; 🚌6, 7, 33, 37, 43, Ⓜ N)

Martuni's LGBTIQ+

16 🚇 MAP P152, G4

Slip behind the velvet curtains into the city's top piano bar, where the rainbow spectrum of regulars seems to have memorized the words to every show tune. Comedy nights are a blast and sing-alongs a given – especially after a couple of top-notch watermelon, pepper-cucumber, lemon-drop or chocolate martinis under $10. Straight-friendly, especially if you sing from the heart. (☎415-241-0205; 4 Valencia St; ⏰4pm-2am; 🚌6, 7, Ⓜ Van Ness)

Entertainment

SFJAZZ Center JAZZ

17 ⭐ MAP P152, H2

Jazz legends and singular talents from Argentina to Yemen are showcased at America's largest jazz center. Hear fresh takes on classic jazz albums and poets riffing with jazz combos in the downstairs Joe Henderson Lab, and witness extraordinary mainstage collaborations by legendary Afro-Cuban All Stars, raucous all-women mariachis Flor de Toluache, and Balkan barnstormers Goran Bregović and his Wedding and Funeral Orchestra. (☎866-920-5299; www.sfjazz.org; 201 Franklin St; tickets $25-120; 👫; 🚌5, 6, 7, 21, 47, 49, Ⓜ Van Ness)

Victorian Color

The city's signature architectural style was labeled 'Victorian,' but demure Queen Victoria would surely blush to see the eccentric architecture perpetrated in her name in San Francisco. Few of the older buildings you'll see in SF were actually built during Victoria's 1837–1901 reign, except for a few rather stern, steeply gabled Gothic Revivals.

The rest of San Francisco's 'Victorians' are cheerfully inauthentic Californian takes on a vaguely Anglo-Continental style, with rococo flourishes that made mansions and bordellos look alike. Local legend has it that to help patrons recognize bordellos, theater masks were incorporated into garland decorations. You'll spot many masks grinning and frowning above windows and doors around Alamo Sq – if those walls could talk, San Francisco might scandalize the world even more than it already does.

When prospectors struck it rich in the gold rush, they upgraded from downtown tenements to grand houses embellished to the eaves with woodwork and gilding. These ornaments served a practical purpose: rows of houses were hastily constructed using a similar template, and citizens needed to know which stairs to stumble up after wild Barbary Coast nights.

From the late 19th to the early 20th century, California's lumber boom produced rows of 'Painted Lady' homes with candy-color palettes, gingerbread woodwork under peaked roofs, and gilded stucco garlands swagging wraparound, look-at-me bay windows. The 1906 quake and fire destroyed many historic buildings east of Van Ness Ave – and much of San Francisco's kitschy, colorful charm went up in smoke.

The 1970s brought a Victorian revival, with Castro house painters leading the Colorist Movement to restore Painted Ladies to their full glory. But as the San Francisco tech economy boomed in the 1990s, their wild six-to-10-color schemes were not as appealing to newly minted millionaires as they had been a century earlier. Many Painted Ladies are now painted historically incorrect but marketable, minimalist white. Alamo Sq mansions currently go for $3 million to $8 million, in case you're in the market.

Booksmith

LIVE PERFORMANCE

18 ⭐ MAP P152, F5

Throw a stone in SF and you'll probably hit a writer (ouch) or reader (ouch again) headed to/from Booksmith. Literary figures organize Booksmith book signings, raucous poetry readings, extra-short fiction improv, and politician-postcard-writing marathons. Head to sister shop-salon-bar the Bindery (1727 Haight St) for boozy book swaps, comedy nights, and silent reading parties hosted by Daniel Handler (aka Lemony Snicket). (📞415-863-8688; www.booksmith.com; 1644 Haight St; events free-$25; 🕙10am-10pm Mon-Sat, to 8pm Sun; ; 🚌6, 7, 43, Ⓜ N)

Independent

LIVE MUSIC

19 ⭐ MAP P152, A3

Bragging rights are earned with breakthrough shows at the small but mighty Independent, hosting DJs and comedians plus indie dreamers (Juana Molina, Death Cab for Cutie), hiphop hitmakers (Ghostface Killah, Janelle Monáe), and genre-defiers (George Clinton, Green Day). Ventilation isn't great in this max-capacity-800, 21+ venue, but the sound is stellar, bathrooms improbably clean, and reasonably priced drinks served in compostable cups. (📞415-771-1421; www.theindependentsf.com; 628 Divisadero St; tickets $12-45; 🕙box office 11am-6pm Mon-Fri, show nights to 9:30pm; 🚌5, 6, 7, 21, 24)

Amoeba Music

Enticements are hardly necessary to lure the masses to the West Coast's most eclectic collection of new and used music and video, but **Amoeba** (Map p152, E6; 📞415-831-1200; www.amoeba.com; 1855 Haight St; 🕙11am-8pm; 🚌6, 7, 33, 43, Ⓜ N) offers listening stations, free zines with uncannily accurate staff reviews, and a free concert series that has starred Billy Bragg, Karl Denson's Tiny Universe, Violent Femmes, and Mike Doughty – plus a foundation that's saved one million acres of rainforest.

Club Deluxe

JAZZ

20 ⭐ MAP P152, G5

Blame it on the bossa nova or the ginned-up Deluxe Spa Collins – you'll be swinging before the night is through. Nightly jazz combos bring the zoot suits and Lindy-Hoppers to the dance floor. Expect mood lighting, cats who wear hats well and dames who can swill $7 happy-hour highballs (4pm to 7pm weekdays, 2pm to 5pm weekends) without losing their matte-red lipstick. (📞415-555-1555; www.clubdeluxe.co; 1511 Haight St; cover free-$10; 🕙4pm-2am Mon-Fri, 2pm-2am Sat & Sun; 🚌6, 7, 33, 37, 43)

Shopping

Bound Together Anarchist Book Collective

BOOKS

21 🔒 MAP P152, H5

Since 1976 this volunteer-run, nonprofit anarchist bookstore has kept free thinkers supplied with organic-permaculture manuals, prison literature, and radical comics, all while coordinating the annual spring Anarchist Book Fair and expanding the *Anarchists of the Americas* storefront mural – makes us tools of the state look like slackers. Hours are impressively regular, but call ahead to be sure. (📞415-431-8355; http://boundtogetherbooks.wordpress.com; 1369 Haight St; 🕐11:30am-7:30pm; 🚌6, 7, 33, 37, 43)

Amour Vert

FASHION & ACCESSORIES

22 🔒 MAP P152, G2

Looking smart comes easily with effortless wardrobe essentials that casually blend style, comfort, and sustainability. Wear your heart on your sleeve with feel-good fabrics ingeniously engineered from renewable sources, including Italian flax linen, beechwood modal, eucalyptus-tree Tencel and cooperative-grown organic cotton. Find soft, flattering pieces at down-to-earth prices, designed in San Francisco and made locally to last a lifetime. (📞415-800-8576;

https://amourvert.com; 437 Hayes St; 🕐11am-7pm Sun-Thu, to 8pm Fri & Sat; 🚌5, 21, 47, 49, Ⓜ Van Ness)

Isotope

COMICS

23 🔒 MAP P152, G2

Toilet seats signed by famous cartoonists over the front counter show just how seriously Isotope takes comics. Newbies tentatively flip through superhero serials, while superfans eye the latest limited-edition graphic novels and head upstairs to lounge with local cartoonists – some of whom teach comics classes here. Don't miss signings and epic over-21 launch parties. (📞415-621-6543; www.isotopecomics.com; 326 Fell St; 🕐11am-7pm Tue-Fri, to 6pm Sat & Sun; ♿; 🚌5, 21, 47, 49)

Wasteland

VINTAGE, CLOTHING

24 🔒 MAP P152, F5

Take center stage in this converted-cinema vintage superstore in barely worn designer rompers, vintage concert tees and a steady supply of go-go boots. Hip occasionally verges on hideous with sequined sweaters and '80s power suits, but, at reasonable (not bargain) prices, anyone can afford fashion risks. If you've got excess baggage, Wasteland buys clothes noon to 6pm daily. (📞415-863-3150; www.shopwasteland.com; 1660 Haight St; 🕐11am-8pm Mon-Sat, to 7pm Sun; 🚌6, 7, 33, 37, 43, ⓂN)

Explore ⊕
Golden Gate Park & the Avenues

Hardcore surfers and gourmet adventurers meet in the foggy Avenues around Golden Gate Park. This is one totally chill global village, featuring bluegrass and Korean BBQ, disc golf and tiki cocktails, French pastries and cult-movie matinees. Beyond the park, time seems to slow down, with the tranquil, mostly residential avenues stretching out toward Ocean Beach.

The Short List

○ **Golden Gate Park (p164)** Skipping, lolling or Lindy-Hopping through America's most outlandish stretch of urban wilderness.

○ **De Young Museum (p165)** Following Andy Goldsworthy's sidewalk fault lines to discover groundbreaking global art.

○ **California Academy of Sciences (p165)** Enjoying sunsets on the wildflower-topped roof and wild evenings at 21-plus NightLife events.

○ **Coastal Trail (p170)** Glimpsing seals, sunsets and shipwrecks along San Francisco's wild waterfront walk.

○ **Ocean Beach (p171)** Numbing your toes in the Pacific and expanding your horizons to Asia over bonfires in artist-designed firepits.

Getting There & Around

🚌 1, 5, 6, 7, 18, 21, 28, 29, 31, 33, 38, 44

Streetcar The N line runs from downtown through the Sunset to Ocean Beach.

Neighborhood Map on p168

California Academy of Sciences (p165)

Top Experience 📷

Meander Through Golden Gate Park

When San Franciscans refer to 'the park,' there's only one that gets the definite article: Golden Gate Park. Everything they hold dear is here: free spirits, free music, redwoods, Frisbee, protests, fine art, bonsai and bison.

◉ MAP P168, D4

https://goldengatepark.
com

btwn Stanyan St & Great
Hwy

admission free

🅿️ 🚻

🚌 5, 7, 18, 21, 28, 29, 33,
44, Ⓜ️ N

Meander Through Golden Gate Park

De Young Museum

The oxidized-copper building may keep a low profile, but there's no denying the park's all-star attraction: the **de Young Museum** (☎415-750-3600; http://deyoung.famsf.org; 50 Hagiwara Tea Garden Dr; adult/child $15/free, 1st Tue of month free; ◷9:30am-5:15pm Tue-Sun; ☐5, 7, 44, Ⓜ N), pictured left. The cross-cultural collection featuring African masks and Turkish kilims alongside California crafts and avant-garde American art has been broadening artistic horizons for a century, and its acclaimed building by Swiss architects Herzog & de Meuron (of Tate Modern fame) is suitably daring.

The 144ft sci-fi **observation tower** is one futuristic feature that seems incongruous with the park setting – but access to the 360-degree tower viewing room is free, and Ruth Asawa's mesmerizing filigreed pods make elevator waits worthwhile.

California Academy of Sciences

Leave it to San Francisco to dedicate a glorious four-story monument entirely to freaks of nature: the **California Academy of Sciences** (☎415-379-8000; www.calacademy. org; 55 Music Concourse Dr; adult/student/child $35.95/30.95/25.95; ◷9:30am-5pm Mon-Sat, from 11am Sun; P ♿; ☐5, 6, 7, 21, 31, 33, 44, Ⓜ N). The Academy's tradition of weird science dates from 1853, with thousands of live animals and 100 research scientists now under a 2.5-acre wildflower-covered roof. Butterflies alight on visitors in the glass **Osher Rainforest Dome**, penguins paddle the tank in the **African Hall**, and Claude the albino alligator stalks the **mezzanine swamp**. Glimpse infinity in the **Morrison Planetarium** and ride the elevator to the blooming Living Roof for park panoramas, before checking out the Giants of Land and Sea exhibit, where you can brave an earthquake

★ Top Tips

○ John F Kennedy Dr is closed to motor vehicles east of Crossover Dr (around 8th Ave) all day Sunday and Saturday mornings to accommodate runners, skateboarders, unicyclists and meandering dreamers.

○ Don't attempt to visit everything in this huge park in a single day; it's more rewarding and relaxing to take in a few sights at a leisurely pace.

✕ Take a Break

○ For quick bites in Golden Gate Park, look for hot-dog carts along John F Kennedy Dr and street-food trucks near the de Young Museum and California Academy of Sciences.

○ For a serviceable sit-down meal inside the park, Beach Chalet (p174) is a reasonable option.

simulation, virtually climb a redwood and get lost in a fog room.

Night owls party on at the Academy's adult after-hours events, where nature-themed cocktails are served and strange mating rituals observed (ID required; $15 entry; 6pm to 10pm Thursday).

San Francisco Botanical Garden

Sniff your way around the world inside the 55-acre **San Francisco Botanical Garden** (Strybing Arboretum; 415-661-1316; www.sfbg.org; 1199 9th Ave; adult/child $9/2, before 9am daily & 2nd Tue of month free; 7:30am-5pm, extended hours in summer & spring, bookstore 10am-4pm; 6, 7, 44, MN), from South African savanna grasses to Japanese magnolias. Don't miss the California native-plant meadow,

Buddha statue, Japanese Tea Garden

STEVE PREZANT / GETTY IMAGES ©

redwood grove and **Ancient Planet Garden**, with plants dating back to California's dinosaur days. **Free tours** take place daily; for details, stop by the bookstore inside the entrance. Last entry is one hour before closing.

Japanese Tea Garden

Since 1894 this 5-acre **garden** (415-752-1171; www.japanese teagardensf.com; 75 Hagiwara Tea Garden Dr; adult/child $8/2, before 10am Mon, Wed & Fri free; 9am-6pm Mar-Oct, to 4:45pm Nov-Feb; P; 5, 7, 44, MN) has blushed pink with cherry blossoms in spring, turned flaming red with maple leaves in fall and induced visitors to lose all track of time in its meditative **Zen Garden**. The century-old **bonsai grove** was cultivated by the Hagiwara family, who returned from WWII Japanese American internment camps to discover that many of their prized miniature evergreens had been sold – and spent decades recovering the precious trees.

Conservatory of Flowers

Flower power is alive and well at SF's **Conservatory of Flowers** (415-831-2090; www.conservatoryofflowers. org; 100 John F Kennedy Dr; adult/student/child $9/6/3, 1st Tue of month free; 10am-6pm Tue-Sun; 5, 7, 21, 33, MN). Inside this gloriously restored 1878 Victorian greenhouse, orchids command center stage like opera divas, lilies float contemplatively in ponds, and gluttonous carnivorous plants gulp down insects.

Outside you'll find the **Dahlia Garden** (www.conservatoryofflowers. org; admission free; ☉sunrise-sunset; 🚻; 🚌5, 21, 33) and its spiky, in-your-face neon blooms cultivated by the city's many hardcore dahlia devotees. The flowers burst onto the scene each June and reach peak punk-rock glory in August or September.

Stow Lake

A park within the park, **Stow Lake** (www.sfrecpark.org; ☉5am-midnight; 🚌7, 44, Ⓜ N) is the place to come for waterfall views, picnics in the **Taiwanese pagoda** and bird-watching on a picturesque island called **Strawberry Hill**. Pedal boats and rowboats are available daily in good weather at the 1946 **boathouse** (📞415-386-2531; http:// stowlakeboathouse.com; 50 Stow Lake Dr; boats per hour $22.50-38.50; ☉10am-5pm; 🚌5, 7, 29, 44). Ghost-hunters come at night seeking the **White Lady** – legend has it she has haunted Stow Lake for a century, searching these shores for her lost child.

Buffalo Paddock

Since 1899 this has been Golden Gate Park's **home where the buffalo roam** (www.golden-gate-park. com/buffalo-paddock.html; admission free; ☉sunrise-sunset; 🚌5, 21) – though technically, they're bison. SF's mellow, well-fed herd rarely moves – but when their tails point upwards, you may be about to witness bison bucking. On the very rare occasion of a stampede, they can reach speeds of up to 30mph. The paddock is off John F Kennedy Dr, near 39th Ave.

National AIDS Memorial Grove

This tranquil, 10-acre **memorial grove** (📞415-765-0446; www. aidsmemorial.org; Bowling Green Dr; admission free; ☉sunrise-sunset; 🚌44, 71, Ⓜ N), graced with poetic paving-stone tributes, was founded in 1991 to commemorate millions of lives lost to the AIDS epidemic and to strengthen national resolve for compassionate care and a lasting cure. Volunteer work days (8:30am to 12:30pm) are held the third Saturday of each month, March to October.

Children's Playground

Kids have had the run of the park's southeastern end since 1887. Highlights of this historic **children's playground** (Koret Children's Quarter; 📞415-831-2700; www. golden-gate-park.com/childrens-playground.html; carousel per ride adult/child $2/1; ☉sunrise-sunset, carousel 10am-4:15pm; 🚻; 🚌7,33, Ⓜ N) include 1970s concrete slides, a climbing wall and a vintage 1912 carousel.

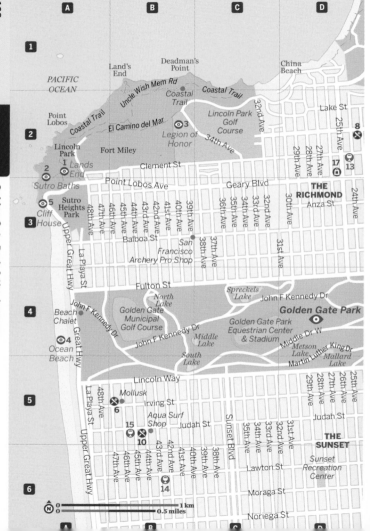

1

2

3

4

5

6

PACIFIC OCEAN

Land's End

Deadman's Point

China Beach

Lake St

Coastal Trail

Uncle Wish Mem Rd

Coastal Trail

Coastal Trail

32nd Ave

Point Lobos

El Camino del Mar

Lincoln Park Golf Course

◎3
Legion of Honor

34th Ave

25th Ave

27th Ave
28th Ave
29th Ave

⊙8
⊙13

Lincoln Park

Fort Miley

Clement St

THE RICHMOND

Geary Blvd

36th Ave
35th Ave
34th Ave
33rd Ave
32nd Ave

30th Ave

⊙17

24th Ave

⊙2
◎1 Lands End
Sutro Baths

Point Lobos Ave

Anza St

◎5
Cliff House

Sutro Heights Park

48th Ave
47th Ave
46th Ave
45th Ave
44th Ave
43rd Ave
42nd Ave
41st Ave
40th Ave
39th Ave

Balboa St

37th Ave
38th Ave

San Francisco Archery Pro Shop

31st Ave

Fulton St

North Lake

Spreckels Lake

John F Kennedy Dr

La Playa St

John F Kennedy Dr

Golden Gate Municipal Golf Course

Golden Gate Park

Beach Chalet

John F Kennedy Dr

Middle Lake

Golden Gate Park Equestrian Center & Stadium

Metson Lake

Middle Dr W

Martin Luther King Dr

Mallard Lake

29th Ave
28th Ave
27th Ave
26th Ave
25th Ave

Great Hwy

◎4
Ocean Beach

South Lake

Lincoln Way

Upper Great Hwy

48th Ave

Mollusk

Irving St

⊗6

31st Ave
32nd Ave
33rd Ave
34th Ave
35th Ave

Judah St

THE SUNSET

Sunset Blvd

⊙15
⊗10

Aqua Surf Shop

Judah St

38th Ave
39th Ave
40th Ave
41st Ave
42nd Ave
43rd Ave
44th Ave
45th Ave
46th Ave
47th Ave

Sunset Recreation Center

Lawton St

⊕14

Moraga St

Noriega St

Ⓝ 0 _____ 1 km
0 _____ 0.5 miles

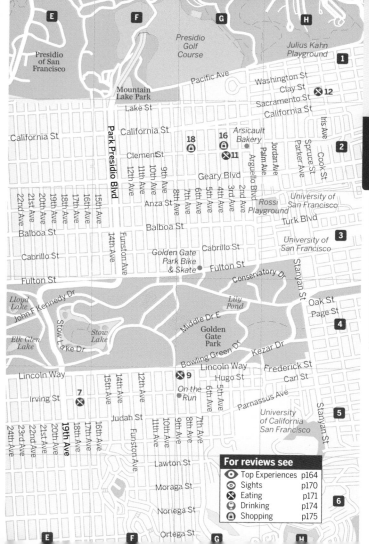

For reviews see

⦿	Top Experiences	p164
◉	Sights	p170
⊗	Eating	p171
⊕	Drinking	p174
⦿	Shopping	p175

Sights

Lands End

PARK

1 ◉ MAP P168, A2

Looking out from Lands End feels like surveying the edge of the world. Nestled on the point of land between Golden Gate Park and the Presidio, the park's hiking trails cross the rugged landscape with alternating ocean vistas and views of the Golden Gate Bridge. The Lands End visitor center and cafe are located at Point Lobos Ave and Merrie Way, overlooking the Sutro Bath ruins. (☎415-426-5240; www.nps.gov; 680 Point Lobos Ave; ☉24hr; ☐38)

Sutro Baths

PARK

2 ◉ MAP P168, A2

It's hard to imagine from these ruins, but Victorian dandies and working stiffs once converged here for bracing baths in woolen rental swimsuits. Millionaire Adolph Sutro built hot and cold indoor pools to accommodate 10,000 unwashed souls in 1896, but the masses apparently preferred dirt – despite added attractions including trapezes and Egyptian mummies, the baths went bust in 1952. At low tide, follow the steep path past the now-ruined baths and through the sea-cave tunnel to find sublime Pacific panoramas. (www.nps.gov/goga/historyculture/sutro-baths.htm; 680 Point Lobos Ave; admission free; ☉sunrise-sunset, visitor center 9am-5pm; P; ☐5, 31, 38)

Coastal Trail

Hit your stride on this 10.5-mile **stretch** (Map p168, B1; www.californiacoastaltrail.info; ☉sunrise-sunset; ☐1, 18, 38), starting at Fort Funston, crossing 4 miles of sandy Ocean Beach and wrapping around the Presidio to the Golden Gate Bridge. Casual strollers can pick up the restored trail near Sutro Baths and head around the Lands End bluffs for end-of-the-world views and glimpses of shipwrecks at low tide.

Legion of Honor

MUSEUM

3 ◉ MAP P168, B2

A museum as eccentric and illuminating as San Francisco itself, the Legion showcases a wildly eclectic collection ranging from Monet water lilies to John Cage soundscapes, ancient Iraqi ivories to R Crumb comics. Upstairs are blockbuster shows of old masters and Impressionists, but don't miss selections from the Legion's Achenbach Foundation of Graphic Arts collection of 90,000 works on paper, ranging from Rembrandt to Ed Ruscha. Ticket price includes free same-day entry to the de Young Museum (p165). (☎415-750-3600; http://legionofhonor.famsf.org; 100 34th Ave; adult/child $15/free, discount with Muni ticket $2, 1st Tue of month free; ☉9:30am-5:15pm Tue-Sun; ☐1, 2, 18, 38)

Ocean Beach

BEACH

4 ⊙ MAP P168, A4

The sun sets over the Pacific just beyond the fog at this blustery beach. Most days are too chilly for bikini-clad clambakes but fine for hardy beachcombers and hardcore surfers braving riptides (casual swimmers, beware). Ocean Beach allows bonfires in 16 artist-designed firepits until 9:30pm; no alcohol permitted. Stick to paths in the fragile southern dunes, where skittish snowy plover shorebirds shelter in winter. (☎415-561-4323; www.parksconservancy.org; Great Hwy; ☺sunrise-sunset; P; ☒5, 18, 31, Ⓜ N)

Cliff House

LANDMARK

5 ⊙ MAP P168, A3

Populist millionaire Adolph Sutro imagined the Cliff House as a working man's paradise in 1863, but Sutro's dream has been rebuilt three times. The latest reworking, a $19-million 2004 facelift, turned the Cliff House into a largely generic, if panoramic, complex housing two restaurants, two bars, two lounges and a gift shop. The key attractions remain: sea lions barking on **Seal Rocks** and the **Camera Obscura**, a vintage 1946 attraction projecting sea views onto a parabolic screen. (☎415-386-3330; www.cliffhouse.com; 1090 Point Lobos Ave; admission free; ☺9am-10:30pm Mon-Thu, to 11:30pm Fri & Sat, 8:30am-9:30pm Sun; ☒5, 18, 31, 38)

Eating

Hook Fish Co

SEAFOOD $

6 ✕ MAP P168, B5

There's a reason you packed that puffy coat: to visit this delightful fish joint out in the windy abyss also known as the Outer Sunset. Order over a small wooden counter from a short menu of locally sourced seafood, including a poke burrito, trout salad and an array of fish-of-the-day tacos, grilled or fried (choose grilled) on warm corn tortillas. (www.hookfishco.com; 4542 Irving St; mains $13-16; ☺11:30am-9pm Mon-Fri, from 9am Sat & Sun; ☒18, Ⓜ N)

King of Noodles

NOODLES $

7 ✕ MAP P168, E5

It's no surprise that the late, great Anthony Bourdain once dropped by this casual dim sum and noodle establishment, where the menu features oddities like marinated pork elbow, black fungus with fresh cucumber and crispy lotus roots (these are amazing, BTW). But it's the delicious hand-pulled noodles in flavorful soups that draw people back, along with the outstanding onion pancakes and the classic Shanghai dumplings. (☎415-566-8318; 1639 Irving St; dim sum $6-9.50, noodles $8-11; ☺11:30am-3:30pm & 5-9:30pm Mon, Tue & Thu; ☒7, 28, 29, Ⓜ N)

Gearing Up for Ocean Beach & Golden Gate Park

Mollusk (Map p168, B5; ☑ 415-564-6300; www.mollusksurfshop.com; 4500 Irving St; ⏰10am-6:30pm Mon-Sat, to 6pm Sun; ☐18, M N) Legendary shapers (surfboard makers) create limited-edition boards and signature T-shirts for this store.

Aqua Surf Shop (Map p168, B5; ☑ 415-242-9283; www.aquasurfshop. com; 3847 Judah St; rental per day bodyboard/wetsuit $10/15, surfboard $25-35; ⏰10am-5:30pm Sun-Tue, to 7pm Wed-Sat; ☐18, M N) Earn Sunset street cred the hardcore way, with Aqua's rental surf gear plus referrals for surf instructors (see website).

On the Run (Map p168, G5; ☑ 415-682-2042; www.ontherunshoes.com; 1310 9th Ave; ⏰10am-7pm Mon-Fri, to 6pm Sat, 11am-6pm Sun; ☐6, 7, 43, 44, M N) If your morning jog leaves your feet or shins hurting, get your gait checked here before you hit Ocean Beach or Golden Gate Park trails.

Golden Gate Park Bike & Skate (Map p168, G3; ☑ 415-668-1117; www. goldengateparkbikeandskate.com; 3038 Fulton St; skates per hour $5-6, per day $20-24, bikes per hour $3-5, per day $15-25, tandem bikes per hour/ day $15/75, discs per hour/day $6/25; ⏰10am-6pm Mon-Fri, to 7pm Sat & Sun; 👪; ☐5, 21, 31, 44) Besides bikes and skates, this rental shop just outside Golden Gate Park offers disc putters and drivers for the park's free Frisbee golf course.

San Francisco Archery Pro Shop (Map p168, B3; ☑ 415-751-2776; www.bysel.com/sfarch; 3795 Balboa St; ⏰11am-6pm; ☐5, 18, 31, 38) Rents and sells bows, arrows and other accessories just a few blocks from the Golden Gate archery range.

Pearl 6101   MEDITERRANEAN $$

8 ❌ MAP P168, D2

Stop by this little neighborhood gem for coffee and wood-fired bagels on your way to the Presidio, or return in the evening for unmissable martinis. Start with some *hamachi crudo* (raw fish) and Miyagi oysters, continue with handmade spaghetti or pork chops, and if your party is large enough, splurge on the massive shared plate of toma-hawk rib-eye chop. (☑415-592-9777; www.pearl6101.com; 6101 California St; mains $19-28; ⏰8am-2pm Tue-Fri, 10am-2pm Sat & Sun, 5-10pm Tue-Sun; ☐1, 2, 29, 38)

Nopalito   MEXICAN $$

9 ❌ MAP P168, G5

Head south of Golden Gate Park's border for upscale, sustainably sourced Cal-Mex, including succulent grass-fed beef empanadas, melt-in-your-mouth carnitas (beer-braised pork) with hand-made organic-corn tortillas, and cinnamon-laced Mexican hot chocolate. Reservations aren't accepted – at sunny weekends when every park-goer craves margaritas and ceviche, show up well in advance to join the paper wait list. ([📞]415-233-9966; www.nopalitosf.com; 1224 9th Ave; mains $13-21; [🕐]11:30am-10pm; [🖋]; [🚌]6, 7, 43, 44, [Ⓜ]N)

Outerlands
CALIFORNIAN $$

10 [✕] MAP P168, B5

When windy Ocean Beach leaves you feeling shipwrecked, drift into this chic beach bistro for organic Californian comfort food. Brunch demands Dutch pancakes baked in a cast iron pan, while lunch calls for pork belly sandwiches and citrusy beach cocktails. Dinner means creative regional fare like Washington manila clams and California Holstein coulotte steak. Reserve. ([📞]415-661-6140; www.outerlandssf.com; 4001 Judah St; sandwiches & small plates $8-14, mains $15-28; [🕐]9am-3pm & 5-10pm; [🖋]; [🚌]18, [Ⓜ]N)

Wako
JAPANESE $$$

11 [✕] MAP P168, G2

Chef-owner Tomoharu Nakamura's driftwood-paneled bistro is as quirkily San Franciscan as the bonsai grove at the nearby Japanese Tea Garden (p166). Each *omakase* (chef's choice) dish is a miniature marvel of Japanese seafood with

Arsicault Bakery

Armando Lacayo left his job in finance because he, like his Parisian grandparents before him, was obsessed with making croissants. After perfecting his technique, Lacayo opened a modest **bakery** (Map p168, G2; [📞]415-750-9460; 397 Arguello Blvd; pastries $3-7; [🕐]7am-2:30pm Mon-Fri, to 3:30pm Sat & Sun; [🚌]1, 2, 33, 38, 44) in the Inner Richmond in 2015. Within a year, *Bon Appétit* magazine had declared it the best new bakery in America and the golden, flaky, buttery croissants regularly sell out. Since then a second location has opened near the Civic Center.

a California accent – Santa Cruz abalone *nigiri* (sushi), seared tuna belly with California caviar, crab *mushimono* (steamed crab) with yuzu grown by a neighbor. *Domo arigato* (thanks very much), dude. ([📞]415-682-4875; www.sushiwakosf.com; 211 Clement St; 9-course menu $135; [🕐]5:30-10pm Tue-Sat; [🚌]1, 2, 33, 38, 44)

Spruce
CALIFORNIAN $$$

12 [✕] MAP P168, H1

VIP all the way: Baccarat crystal chandeliers, tawny leather chairs, rotating art collections and 2500 wines. Ladies who lunch dispense with polite conversation, tearing into grass-fed burgers on house-baked English muffins loaded with pickled onions and heirloom tomatoes grown on the restaurant's own organic farm. Want fries with that? Oh, yes, you do: Spruce's are cooked in duck fat. (☎415-931-5100; www.sprucesf.com; 3640 Sacramento St; mains $19-44; ⏰11:30am-2pm & 5-10pm Mon-Thu, 11:30am-2pm & 5-11pm Fri, 10am-2pm & 5-11pm Sat, 10am-2pm & 5-9pm Sun; 🚌1, 2, 33, 43)

Drinking

Violet's Tavern

COCKTAIL BAR

13 🚇 MAP P168, D2

Here's another neighborhood cocktail bar that doubles as a delectable brunch and dinner spot, but the drinks are really where it's at. Case in point, the Siberian Tea Service: a warm concoction of Japanese whiskey, plum wine, oolong tea and hibiscus. Or how about the Violet Skies, with mezcal, strawberry brandy and some crème de violette? (☎415-682-4861; www.violets-sf.com; 2301 Clement St; ⏰bar 5-10:30pm Mon, to 11pm Tue-Thu, to midnight Fri, 11am-midnight Sat, 11am-10pm Sun; 🚌1, 2, 29, 38)

Woods Outbound

CRAFT BEER

On a chilly evening, squeeze into this narrow, cozy craft-beer bar (see 15 🚇 Map p168, B5) and give some inventive brews a try. The brewmasters are known for throwing unusual ingredients into their

Beach Chalet

Microbrews with views: watch Pacific sunsets through pint glasses of the **Beach Chalet's** (Map p168, A4; ☎415-386-8439; www.beachchalet.com; 1000 Great Hwy; ⏰9am-10pm Mon-Thu, to midnight Fri, 8am-midnight Sat, 8am-11pm Sun; 🚌5, 18, 31) Riptide Red ale from the comfort of the formal upstairs dining room. Downstairs, splendid 1930s Works Project Administration (WPA) frescoes celebrate the building of Golden Gate Park. In the backyard, Park Chalet, the casual bar/restaurant, hosts raucous Taco Tuesdays, lazy Sunday brunch, and live music at weekends.

20-gallon brewing system – yerba maté or yams, for instance – and the Morpho herbal ale is an unusual organic favorite. (☎415-571-8025; www.woodsbeer.com/outbound; 4045 Judah St; ⏰4-10pm Mon-Wed, to midnight Thu, 3pm-midnight Fri, noon-midnight Sat, noon-10pm Sun; 🚌18, Ⓜ N)

Andytown Coffee

COFFEE

14 🚇 MAP P168, B6

Since 2014 Andytown Coffee has spread like afternoon fog, unstoppable thanks to its yummy drip coffee, Irish-inspired soda bread and one-of-a-kind 'snowy plover', a delightful concoction of Pellegrino, ice, two shots of espresso and a scoop of whipped cream. In the last few years, outlets have opened on the increasingly hip **Taraval St** (415-571-8052; 3629 Taraval St; ☉7am-5pm; ☎; ☐18, Ⓜ L), and downtown near the Salesforce Transit Center. (415-753-9775; www.andytownsf.com; 3655 Lawton St; ☉7am-5pm; ☎; ☐18, Ⓜ N)

Trouble Coffee Co
CAFE

15 🍴 MAP P168, B5

Coconuts are unlikely near blustery Ocean Beach, but here comes Trouble with the 'Build Your Own Damn House' breakfast special: coffee, thick-cut cinnamon-laced toast and an entire young coconut. Join surfers sipping house roasts on driftwood perches outside, or toss back espresso at the reclaimed-wood counter. Featured on National Public Radio, but not Instagram – sorry, no indoor photos or laptops. (4033 Judah St; ☉7am-7pm; ☐18, Ⓜ N)

Shopping

Park Life
GIFTS & SOUVENIRS

16 🔒 MAP P168, G2

The Swiss Army knife of hip SF emporiums, Park Life is design store, indie publisher and art gallery rolled into one. Browse among presents too clever to give away, including toy soldiers in yoga poses, Park Life catalogs of Shaun O'Dell paintings of natural disorder, sinister Todd Hido photos

of shaggy cats on shag rugs, and a Picasso bong. (415-386-7275; www.parklifestore.com; 220 Clement St; ☉10am-7pm Mon-Sat, to 6pm Sun; ☐1, 2, 33, 38, 44)

Paul's Hat Works
HATS

17 🔒 MAP P168, D2

Psst...keep this SF style secret under your hat: there is no Paul. Started in 1918 by a Peruvian hatmaker named Napoleon, Paul's has been maintained by three generations of 'master hatters' handcrafting noir-novel fedoras on-site. Head downtown in Paul's jazz-standard porkpie, social-climb Nob Hill in Paul's stovepipe top hat or storm Trad'r Sam down the block in Paul's classic panama. (415-221-5332; www.hatworksbypaul.com; 6128 Geary Blvd; ☉10am-3pm Wed-Fri, noon-4pm select Sat; ☐1, 38)

Green Apple Books
BOOKS

18 🔒 MAP P168, G2

Stagger out of this literary opium den while you still can, laden with remaindered art books, used cookbooks and just-released novels signed by local authors. If two floors of bookish bliss aren't enough, check out more new titles, in-store readings and events at Green Apple Books on the Park (1231 9th Ave). (415-387-2272; www.greenapplebooks.com; 506 Clement St; ☉10am-10:30pm; ☐2, 38, 44)

Survival Guide

City skyline view from Coit Tower (p74) RICOWDE / GETTY IMAGES ©

Before You Go

Book Your Stay

o San Francisco hotel rates are among the world's highest. Plan ahead and grab bargains when you see them; note the 15% room tax on top of quoted rates.

o Downtown hotels offer bargain rates, but avoid the sketchy, depressing Tenderloin – the worst area extends three blocks in all directions from Eddy and Jones Sts.

o Hotel parking costs $40 to $60 per night extra – very few offer a free self-service lot.

Useful Websites

BedandBreakfast.com (www.bedandbreak fast.com) Listings include local B&Bs and neighborhood inns.

HotelTonight (www. hoteltonight.com) SF-based hotel-search app offering last-minute discounted bookings.

Lonely Planet (www. lonelyplanet.com/usa/ san-francisco/hotels)

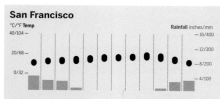

San Francisco
°C/°F Temp
40/104 —
20/68 —
0/32 —
Rainfall inches/mm
— 16/400
— 12/300
— 8/200
— 4/100

When to Go

o **Winter (Dec–Feb)** Low-season rates, brisk but rarely cold days, and the colorful Lunar New Year parade.

o **Spring (Mar–Apr)** Film festivals, blooming parks and mid-season rates make the occasional damp day worthwhile.

o **Summer (May–Aug)** Street fairs, farmers markets and June Pride celebrations compensate for high-season rates and chilly afternoon fog.

o **Fall (Sep–Nov)** Prime time for blue skies, free concerts, better hotel rates and flavor-bursting harvest cuisine.

Recommendations and bookings.

Best Budget

HI San Francisco Fisherman's Wharf (www.hiusa.org) Waterfront hostel with million-dollar views.

San Remo Hotel (www. sanremohotel.com) Spartan furnishings, shared bathrooms, great rates.

Pacific Tradewinds Hostel (www.san-francisco-hostel.com) Downtown hostel with snappy design.

Yotel (www.yotel. com/en/hotels/yotel-san-francisco) Smart downtown digs with shared workspace.

Best Midrange

Inn at the Presidio (www.presidiolodging. com) Small luxury inn surrounded by national-park land.

Hotel Carlton (www. hotelcarltonsf.com) Jet-set vibe with good-value rooms.

Marker (http://the markersanfrancisco. com) Snazzy design, useful amenities and a central location.

White Swan Inn (www. whiteswaninnsf.com) Eccentric and fashion-forward near downtown shopping.

Hotel Kabuki (www. jdvhotels.com) Rockstar hideaway in Japantown.

Hotel Zeppelin (www. viceroyhotelsand resorts.com) Psychedelic SF style in the heart of downtown.

Best Top End

Hotel Drisco (www. hoteldrisco.com) Luxury inn overlooking Marina mansions.

Loews Regency (www. loewshotels.com/ regency-san-francisco) Five-star service and knockout views.

Palace Hotel (www. rycollection.com) This stately classical hotel is also a century-old landmark.

Hotel Zetta (www. hotelzetta.com) Tech-centric downtowner filled with art.

Argonaut Hotel (www.argonauthotel. com) Bay views in a converted Fisherman's Wharf warehouse.

Arriving in San Francisco

San Francisco Airport (SFO)

BART Direct 30-minute ride to/from downtown San Francisco. The SFO BART station is connected to the International Terminal.

Shuttle Bus Airport shuttles (one way $19 to $25) depart from upper-level ticketing areas; anticipate 45 minutes to most SF locations. Companies include SuperShuttle, Quake City and American Airporter Shuttle.

Express bus SamTrans (☎ 800-660-4287; www. samtrans.com) Bus 398 takes 30 to 45 minutes to reach the Salesforce Transit Center (https:// salesforcetransitcenter. com).

Taxis Cost $50 to $65 plus tip and depart from SFO's lower-level baggage-claim area.

Ride-share Fares range from $35 to $60 off-peak for a

direct-to-destination ride. Ride-shares meet curbside at the upstairs Departures level.

Car Downtown San Francisco is a 25- to 60-minute, 14-mile trip north from SFO up Hwy 101.

Oakland International Airport (OAK)

BART BART people-mover shuttles run every 10 to 20 minutes from Terminal 1 to the Coliseum station, where you connect with BART trains to downtown SF ($10.95, 25 minutes).

Shuttle Bus Super-Shuttle (☎ 800-258-3826; www.supershuttle. com) offers shared van rides from OAK to downtown San Francisco for $75 for up to three people (reservation required).

Taxis Taxis leave curbside from OAK and average $35 to $55 to Oakland, $70 to $90 to SF.

San Jose International Airport (SJC)

Caltrain The free **VTA** (Valley Transit Authority;

Transit Passes

Muni Passport (1/3/7 days $23/34/45) allows unlimited travel on all Muni transport, including cable cars. It's sold at the Muni kiosk at the Powell St cable-car turnaround on Market St; SF's Visitor Information Center; the TIX Bay Area kiosk at Union Sq; and shops around town – see www.sfmta.com for exact locations. One-day (but not multiday) passports are available from cable-car conductors.

Clipper Cards Downtown Muni/BART stations have machines that issue the Clipper card (www.clippercard.com), a reloadable transit card that costs $3 with a $2 minimum and can be used on Muni, BART, AC Transit, Caltrain, SamTrans and Golden Gate Transit (but not cable cars). The cards automatically deduct fares and apply transfers – only one Muni fare is deducted per 90-minute period.

☏ 408-321-2300; www.vta.org) Airport Flyer regularly connects the Santa Clara Caltrain station and the airport. From Santa Clara station, Caltrain (one way $10.50, 1½ hours) runs northbound trains to the SF terminus at 4th and King Sts.

Car It's a straight shot to the city via Hwy 101; expect heavy traffic during peak times.

Emeryville Amtrak Station (EMY)

Train Amtrak
(☏ 800-872-7245; www.amtrak.com) serves San Francisco via stations in Oakland and Emeryville, with free shuttle-bus connections to San Francisco's Ferry Building and Caltrain station.

Getting Around

Cable Car

o Frequent, slow and scenic, from 6am to 12:30am daily.

o Cable-car tickets cost $7 per ride, and can be bought at cable-car-turnaround kiosks or on board from the conductor.

o For frequent use, get a Muni Passport ($23 per day).

Streetcar

o Fares are $2.75 cash, or $2.50 with a reloadable Clipper card.

o Streetcars, and particularly lines J, K/T, L, M and N, are often faster than driving.

o Schedules vary by line; infrequent after 9pm.

BART

o High-speed transit to East Bay, Mission St, SF airport and Millbrae, where it connects with Caltrain.

o Within San Francisco, one-way fares start at $2.50.

o The fastest link between downtown and the Mission District also offers transit to SF airport (SFO; $9.65), Oakland ($4) and Berkeley ($4.60).

Bus

o The standard cash fare for buses is $2.75, and

each ticket is good for 120 minutes of travel. With a reloadable Clipper card, discounted fare is $2.50.

○ For route planning and schedules, consult http://transit.511.org.

○ For real-time departures, see www.nextmuni.com. It syncs with GPS on buses to provide best estimates on arrival times.

Taxi

○ Fares are about $3 per mile; meters start at $3.50.

○ For quickest service in San Francisco, download the Flywheel app for smartphones, which dispatches the nearest taxi.

○ Lyft and Uber are available in San Francisco, but licensed taxis have greater access, specifically to dedicated downtown bus and taxi lanes, notably along Market St. Taxis also don't charge surge pricing at peak times.

Bicycle

○ Contact the **San Francisco Bicycle Coalition** (☎415-431-2453; www.sfbike.org) for maps,

information and laws regarding bicyclists.

○ Bicycles can be taken on most Muni buses and some BART trains.

○ **Ford GoBikes** (☎855-480-2453; www.fordgobike.com; single ride/day pass $2/10) are available within SF for single trips, day use or with monthly access passes.

Car

○ Traffic is notoriously bad, and parking is next to impossible. Avoid driving until it's time to leave town.

○ San Francisco streets mostly follow a grid bisected by Market St, with signs pointing toward tourist zones.

○ Before heading to any bridge, airport or other traffic choke-point, call 511 for a traffic update.

Essential Information

Accessible Travel

All Bay Area transit companies offer wheelchair-accessible service and travel discounts for travelers

with disabilities. Major car-rental companies can usually supply hand-controlled vehicles with one or two days' notice. For people with visual impairment, major intersections emit a chirping signal to indicate when it is safe to cross the street.

San Francisco Bay Area Regional Transit Guide (https://511.org/transit/accessibility/overview) Covers accessibility for people with disabilities.

Muni's Street & Transit (www.sfmta.com/accessibility) Details wheelchair-friendly bus routes and streetcar stops.

Independent Living Resource Center of San Francisco (☎415-543-6222, TTY 415-543-6698; www.ilrcsf.org; ⏰9am-4:30pm Mon-Thu, to 4pm Fri) Provides information about wheelchair accessibility on Bay Area public transit and in hotels and other local facilities.

Environmental Traveling Companions (☎415-474-7662; www.etctrips.org) Leads excellent outdoor trips in California –

Money-Saving Tips

o Summer festivals in Golden Gate Park and neighborhood street fairs are often free.

o Many SF museums are free the first Tuesday of the month, and some evening events offer steeply discounted admission; see individual listings.

o Sign up at Gold Star Events (www.goldstar events.com) for discounts on comedy, theater, concerts and opera.

white-water rafting, kayaking and cross-country skiing – for kids with disabilities.

Download Lonely Planet's free Accessible Travel guides from https://shop. lonelyplanet.com/ categories/accessible-travel.com

Business Hours

Typical opening hours in San Francisco:

Banks 9am to 4:30pm or 5pm Monday to Friday, plus occasionally 9am to noon Saturday

Offices 8:30am to 5:30pm Monday to Friday

Restaurants Breakfast 8am to 10am; lunch 11:30am to 2:30pm; dinner 5:30pm, with last service 9pm to 9:30pm

weekdays or 10pm weekends; Saturday and Sunday brunch 10am to 2:30pm

Shops 10am to 6pm or 7pm Monday to Saturday, though hours may run 11am to 8pm Saturday and 11am to 6pm Sunday

Discount Cards

Some green-minded venues, such as the de Young Museum, the California Academy of Sciences and the Legion of Honor, also offer discounts to ticket-bearing Muni riders.

City Pass (www. citypass.com; adult/child $94/74) Covers three days of cable cars and Muni, plus entry to four attractions, including the California Academy of Sciences, Blue & Gold Fleet Bay

Cruise, the Aquarium of the Bay and either the Exploratorium or SFMOMA.

Go Card (www. smartdestinations. com; adult/child one day $74/54, two days $109/89, three days $139/124) Provides access to the city's major attractions, including the California Academy of Sciences, the de Young Museum, the Aquarium of the Bay, SFMOMA, USS Pampanito, the Beat Museum and Exploratorium, plus discounts on packaged tours and waterfront restaurants and cafes.

Electricity

Type A
120V/60Hz

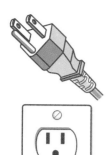

**Type B
120V/60Hz**

Emergencies

Emergency	☎ 911
Non-emergency	☎ 311
San Francisco city/ area code	☎ 415
US country code	☎ 1

LGBTIQ+ Travelers

San Francisco is without doubt one of the most LGBTIQ-friendly cities in the United States. It is home to the world's first gay bar with windows open to the street, as well as America's first LGBITQ+ history museum. SF's DMV officially recognizes trans-queer identities.

Money

ATMs are widely available; credit cards are accepted at most hotels, stores and restaurants. Many farmers-market stalls and food trucks and some bars are cash only. Keep small bills for cafes, bars and hotel service, where cash tips are appreciated.

Changing Money

Though there are exchange bureaus at airports, the best rates are generally in town. You can change money at **Currency Exchange International** (☎ 415-974-6600; www.sanfranciscocurrency exchange.com; 865 Market St, Westfield Centre, Level 1; ⏱ 10am-8:30pm Mon-Sat, 11am-7pm Sun; Ⓜ Powell, Ⓑ Powell) and **Bank of America** (☎ 415-837-1394; www.bankamerica.com; 1 Powell St, downstairs; ⏱ 9am-5pm Mon-Fri, 10am-2pm Sat; Ⓜ Powell, Ⓑ Powell).

Traveler's Checks

In the US, traveler's checks in US dollars are virtually as good as cash; you don't necessarily have to go to a bank to cash them,

as some establishments – particularly hotels – will accept them like cash. Fair warning, though: more SF venues accept Apple Pay than traveler's checks.

Public Holidays

Most shops remain open on public holidays (with the exception of Independence Day, Thanksgiving, Christmas Day and New Year's Day), but banks, schools and offices are usually closed. Holidays that may affect business hours and transit schedules include the following:

Martin Luther King Jr Day Third Monday in January

Presidents' Day Third Monday in February

Easter Sunday (and Good Friday and Easter Monday) in March or April

Memorial Day Last Monday in May

Independence Day July 4

Labor Day First Monday in September

Columbus Day Second Monday in October

Veterans Day
November 11

Thanksgiving Fourth
Thursday in November

Responsible Travel

Go green

○ Stay at California-certified green Orchard Garden Hotel, Hotel del Sol, Inn at the Presidio or Hotel Drisco.

○ Enjoy organic, local fare at SF bars and bistros with curbside parklets – parking spots reclaimed for plants and people, invented in 2010 by Bay Area Rebar Studio.

Give back

○ Love the food? Thank farmers who make it possible at Ferry Building, Castro and Heart of the City farmers markets.

○ Appreciate local hospitality? Pay it forward by volunteering with Glide Memorial, providing 2000+ free meals daily.

○ Collect souvenirs? Shop stores in this guide – all locally owned – and recycle excess at Community Thrift.

Dos & Don'ts

Formality: San Franciscans are extremely informal; there are no special formalities travelers must be aware of. Jeans can be worn almost anywhere – they were invented here.

Greeting: Instead of handshakes, kisses on one or both cheeks are an acceptable alternative and very common in non-COVID times. Hugging is also common among friends, but ask acquaintances and coworkers first to avoid catching them by surprise.

Safe Travel

Keep your city smarts and wits about you, especially at night in the Tenderloin, South of Market (SoMa), the Upper Haight and the Mission. If you're alone in these areas at night, consider ride-share or a taxi instead of waiting for a bus.

○ Avoid using your smartphone unnecessarily on the street – phone-snatching does happen.

○ The Bayview–Hunters Point neighborhood (south of Potrero Hill, along the water) isn't suitable for wandering tourists, due to policing and crime issues.

○ After dark, Mission Dolores Park, Buena Vista Park and the entry to Golden Gate Park at Haight and Stanyan Sts are used for drug deals and casual hookups. If you're there at night, you may get propositioned.

Telephone

The US country code is 📞1. San Francisco's city/area code is 📞415. When calling local numbers in San Francisco you must dial the area code; thus, all local numbers begin with 📞1-415.

To place an international call, dial 📞011 + country code + city code + number (make sure to drop the 0 that precedes foreign city codes or your call won't go through). When calling Canada, there's no need to dial the international access code (📞011). When dialing from a landline, you must precede any area code by 📞1 for direct dialing, 📞0 for collect calls and operator assistance (both expensive); from cell phones, dial only the area code and number.

Area Codes

East Bay 📞510

Marin County 📞415

Peninsula 📞650

San Francisco 📞415

San Jose 📞408

Santa Cruz 📞831

Wine Country 📞707

Toll-free numbers start with 📞800, 855, 866, 877 or 888; phone numbers beginning with 📞900 usually incur high fees.

Operator Services

International operator 📞00

Local directory 📞411

Long-distance directory information 📞1 + area code + 555-1212

Operator 📞0

Toll-free number information 📞800-555-1212

Toilets

Many toilets in public or shared spaces in San Francisco are designated for use by all genders, denoted by a triangle. All-gender toilets usually have stalls instead of urinals.

Citywide Self-cleaning, coin-operated outdoor kiosk commodes cost 25¢ or require a free token to enter; there are 28 citywide, mostly in North Beach, Fisherman's Wharf, the Financial District and the Tenderloin. Toilet paper isn't always available, and there's a 20-minute time limit. Public library branches, including San Francisco Main Library, and some city parks also have restrooms.

Downtown Most hotel lobbies have restrooms. Clean toilets and baby-changing tables can be found at Westfield San Francisco Centre and Macy's.

Haight-Ashbury & Mission District Woefully lacking in public toilets; you may have to buy a drink or food to gain access to locked customer-only bathrooms.

Tourist Information

SF Visitor Information Center (www.sanfrancisco.travel/visitor-information-center) Muni Passports, activities deals, culture and event calendars.

For further tourist information, visit these websites:

SFGate (www.sfgate.com)

SFist (www.sfist.com)

48 Hills (https://48hills.org)

Visas

USA Visa Waiver Program (VWP) allows nationals from 38 countries to enter the US without a visa, provided they are carrying a machine-readable e-passport (with an embedded chip). For the updated list of countries included in the program and current requirements, see the **US Customs & Border Protection** (https://www.cbp.gov/travel/international-visitors/) website.

Citizens of VWP countries need to register with the **US Department of Homeland Security** (https://esta.cbp.dhs/gov/esta) three days before their visit. There is a $14 fee for registration application.

Behind the Scenes

Send Us Your Feedback

We love to hear from travelers – your comments help make our books better. We read every word, and we guarantee that your feedback goes straight to the authors. Visit **lonelyplanet.com/contact** to submit your updates and suggestions.

Note: We may edit, reproduce and incorporate your comments in Lonely Planet products such as guidebooks, websites and digital products, so let us know if you don't want your comments reproduced or your name acknowledged. For a copy of our privacy policy visit lonelyplanet.com/privacy.

Ashley's Thanks

Thanks to my editor Sarah Stocking and to my co-author Alison Bing for all their sound advice and enthusiasm for the project. Thanks to Andy Wright, David Roth, Amy Benziger, Kara Levy, Lauren Smiley, Laurie Prill, Paul Stockamore, Osa Peligrosa, Freda Moon, Lois Beckett, Margie Benziger and Peter Benziger for the friendship and the shared meals and the ideas. Most of all thanks to my amazing boyfriend Steven Sparapani. I love you the absolute most.

Acknowledgements

Cover photograph: Cable car, San Francisco, chuckstock/Shutterstock ©; Back cover photograph: Crosswalk, the Castro, eddie-hernandez.com/Shutterstock ©; Photographs pp26-7 (counterclockwise from left): huangcolin/Shutterstock ©; V_E/Shutterstock ©; wendy connett/Alamy Stock Photo ©; fotoVoyager/Getty Images ©

This Book

This 8th edition of Lonely Planet's *Pocket San Francisco* guidebook was curated by Ashley Harrell, and researched and written by Ashley and Alison Bing. This guidebook was produced by the following:

Destination Editor Sarah Stocking

Senior Product Editors Daniel Bolger, Martine Power, Vicky Smith

Cartographers Julie Dodkins, Valentina Kremenchutskaya, Alison Lyall

Product Editor Clare Healy

Book Designer Hannah Blackie

Assisting Editors Sarah Bailey, Bruce Evans, Gabrielle Innes, Alison Morris, Lauren O'Connell, Fergus O'Shea, Monique Perrin, Gabrielle Stefanos, Sarah Stewart, Monica Woods

Cover Researchers Fergal Condon, Gwen Cotter

Thanks to Ronan Abayawickrema, William Allen, Jane Fletcher, Amy Lynch, Alison Killilea, Angela Tinson

Index

See also separate subindexes for:

⊗ **Eating** p190

◯ **Drinking** p190

✦ **Entertainment** p191

▢ **Shopping** p191

Our Writers

Ashley Harrell

After a brief stint selling day-spa coupons door-to-door in South Florida, Ashley decided she'd rather be a writer. She went to journalism grad school, convinced a newspaper to hire her, and started covering wildlife, crime and tourism, sometimes all in the same story. Fueling her zest for storytelling and the unknown, she traveled widely and moved often, from a tiny NYC apartment to a vast California ranch to a jungle cabin in Costa Rica, where she started writing for Lonely Planet. From there her travels became more exotic and farther flung, and she still laughs when paychecks arrive.

Alison Bing

Over 10 guidebooks and 20 years in San Francisco, Alison has spent more time on Alcatraz than some inmates, become an aficionado of drag and burritos, and willfully ignored Muni signs warning that safety requires avoiding unnecessary conversation.

Published by Lonely Planet Global Limited
CRN 554153
8th edition – March 2022
ISBN 978 1 78868 406 4
© Lonely Planet 2022 Photographs © as indicated 2022
10 9 8 7 6 5 4 3 2 1
Printed in Malaysia